PALEO COOKING

WITH YOUR

80+ RECIPES FOR HEALTHIER FRIED FOOD IN LESS TIME

DR. KAREN S. LEE

**Founder of
www.drkarenslee.com**

PAGE STREET
PUBLISHING CO.

First published in 2018 by
Page Street Publishing Co.
27 Congress Street, Suite 105
Salem, MA 01970
www.pagestreetpublishing.com

Distributed by Macmillan, sales in Canada by The Canadian Manda Group.

22   21   20   19   18   1   2   3   4   5

ISBN-13: 978-1-62414-611-4
ISBN-10: 1-62414-611-2

Library of Congress Control Number: 2018932225

Cover and book design by Page Street Publishing Co.
Photography by Donna Crous

Printed and bound in China

To my husband, for being willing to try anything once, maybe twice, and for believing in my method of madness.

To my children, whose unfortunate health issues made me into a better researcher, investigator and detective. And like your dad, for your gastronomic curiosities, allowing me to explore cooking adventures in the kitchen, and making me a published cookbook author.

I dedicate this book to *you.*

Contents

INTRODUCTION

As a doctor of chiropractics, I educated my patients about their health across many aspects, including proper ergonomics, food and nutrition. Their physical health improved only when their intake of the right foods and nutrients improved. So it pained me a great deal when my children became affected by food allergies and sensitivities, manifested as respiratory distress and eczema.

I sought to help my children's allergies by putting them on an elimination diet, but it wasn't until they started on the Paleo diet that they began to heal. And my husband and I became accidental beneficiaries when we didn't want to taunt them by eating what they couldn't eat in front of them. We were the "Parents of the Year," after all. Okay, that's a lie. I was too "lazy" to cook two separate meals, so we ended up on the Paleo diet by default. But it was the best decision we made—we became leaner and stronger as our children's health improved.

I wasn't always so obsessed with food. Obsessed with eating, yes, but not with avoiding or substituting ingredients when cooking, since I always cooked with real ingredients without excessive amounts of sugar. I've been trained to think of food as medicine (or poison to some, as some foods are to my children), but gut-related issues can be very difficult to diagnose when the symptoms are not always obvious. This fact was proven right before my eyes when my daughter contracted a stomach virus one day in high school. She could not keep anything down and all she could manage not to vomit was a plain rice porridge and a little bit of kimchi juice. After a week of eating nothing but those two foods, her long-standing eczema totally cleared up, at least during this bout with gastroenteritis. That's when I confirmed my gut feeling that her skin problem was connected to food allergies, a connection her pediatrician always denied.

As miraculous as the Paleo eating style was, someone—mainly me—had to plan, shop and cook the meals. With an increasingly hectic schedule, shopping for fresh ingredients is challenging enough, but making grain-free and dairy-free foods taste as good as the conventional ones is tricky. Furthermore, foods that we used to enjoy, like fried foods, had to be cooked in a different method to taste the way we remember. That is hard. I mean, let's be honest; baked fries or chicken is okay, but they are not the same as deep-fried. Am I right? I had to utilize all the practical kitchen appliances, like the air fryer, to my advantage to satisfy my family's unapologetic love for good-tasting food.

My kitchen is on the small-ish side and I hate clutter. When my daughter told me about the air fryer, I cringed at the thought of one more kitchen appliance on the counter and ignored her suggestion. Since I cook mostly Paleo, deep-fried food was almost never on the menu, and I couldn't justify buying it just to fry foods. But that was two years ago. Now that I've been using the air fryer on a regular basis, I'm asking myself: Why didn't I listen to my daughter before? But as they say, it's better late than never, right?

Paleo Cooking with Your Air Fryer is a collection of my "Paleotized" recipes using the air fryer for frying without using a pot of sizzling hot oil. These recipes (some are methods rather than recipes) will make you look like the best cook in the world while using less oil and without deep frying. Don't get me wrong; cooking with oil is okay, as long as it's a good quality oil like avocado or extra-virgin olive oil. But using it to deep-fry food all the time is less than desirable for your gut. The air fryer uses a fan to circulate the heated air to fry, bake, broil and roast in the confined space of a little oven that takes up no more counter space than a bread box. And let's face it. We all need to indulge once in a while without compromising our health, right? Well, this book will show you how to make fried chicken (Not Your Gramma's Fried Chicken, page 76), crispy veggies (Fancy Pants French Fries, page 118; Vegetable Tempura, page 127) and healthy nourishing treats (Simple Chocolate Mud Cake, page 149), baked in a jiffy to satiate your cravings.

Who says you can't enjoy fried food when you're on a Paleo diet? Not me! With the air fryer, you can eat great tasting food without compromising your health. And the air fryer makes cooking so much easier and quicker, so it makes cooking fun again. Here's to healthy frying!

In Your Health,

—Karen Lee, D.C.

WHET YOUR PALATE

Who says appetizers have to be served only in restaurants and at parties? When your family is whining because they are hungry and rummaging the fridge for food, these finger foods will shut them up so fast that they'll wonder why they were complaining. Make these in advance, freeze them and reheat in the air fryer to silence them instantly. You can thank me later as you set the table for a nice, quiet family dinner. Or maybe not, because your family may not even want the entrees! And who would blame them because some of the classic hors d'oeuvres have been jazzed up with modern twists, like Healthy Korean Chicken Wings (page 11), Oysters Rockefeller (page 12) and Kimchi Deviled Eggs (page 19). And no one will know the Stuffed Portobello Mushrooms (page 15) are Paleo, even the non-Paleo folks.

Healthy KOREAN CHICKEN WINGS

Korean spices make these chicken wings different from other spicy chicken wings. You could possibly substitute the gochugaru and gochujang with other peppery sauces but then you will miss out on its unique taste. If you can't find these two ingredients near you, check Amazon. Just make sure it is wheat-free gochujang. You will be glad you took the extra effort to make these finger-licking-good wings with original Korean spices. Sit with a pitcher of your favorite drink and be ready to be awakened by bursts of hot, sexy flavors!

COOK TIME: 15 MINUTES || SERVINGS: 4

---

16 chicken wings

1 tsp chopped garlic

1 tsp grated fresh ginger

1 tbsp (15 g) gochujang (Korean red pepper paste)

KOREAN CHICKEN WINGS SAUCE

½ tsp sea salt

2 tsp (9 g) gochugaru (Korean red pepper flakes)

1 tbsp (11 g) cayenne pepper

2 tsp (9 g) grated fresh ginger

2 cloves garlic, minced

¼ cup (61 g) gochujang

2 tbsp (30 ml) water

1 tsp sesame oil

½ tsp toasted sesame seeds

1 tsp apple cider vinegar

1 tbsp (15 ml) raw honey

½ tsp toasted sesame seeds, for garnish

1 tbsp (3 g) diagonally sliced scallions, for garnish

Separate the drummettes from the wingettes and discard the tips. Combine the chicken parts with the garlic, ginger and gochujang, and marinate overnight. Make the Korean chicken wings sauce by combining all the ingredients in an airtight container, then refrigerate.

Preheat the air fryer to 360°F (180°C).

Take the wings out of the refrigerator and blot the liquid from the wings with a paper towel. When the air fryer reaches the desired temperature, put the wings in the basket and set the timer for 12 minutes. Shake the basket at the halfway point and turn over any wings that are not browning.

Meanwhile, transfer the marinade to a medium saucepan and simmer on low heat. Reserve 2 tablespoons (30 ml) of the marinade to serve on the side.

When the timer goes off and the wings are brown, transfer all the wings to the pan and coat the wings with the sauce. Return the wings to the air fryer, set the timer for 3 minutes and cook until the timer goes off. Transfer the chicken wings to a plate, sprinkle with sesame seeds and scallions before serving with the sauce on the side.

Oysters ROCKEFELLER

My daughter Emily loves oysters but she thought they were only eaten raw . . . until I made these. Since she's sensitive to gluten, I substituted the flour, customarily used in the green mixture, with almond flour, which adds more depth to the flavor!

COOK TIME: 10 MINUTES + 15–18 MINUTES STOVETOP COOKING || **SERVINGS: 4**

8 live oysters on the half shell

4 tbsp (60 g) ghee

3 strips uncured bacon, finely chopped

⅓ cup (67 g) finely chopped purple onion (reserve 1 tsp for garnish)

2 cloves garlic, minced

½ cup (75 g) finely chopped fresh spring greens (e.g., spinach, kale, arugula, Swiss chard)

⅓ cup (13 g) finely chopped parsley (reserve 1 tsp for garnish)

⅓ cup (32 g) extra fine blanched almond flour

Pinch of salt and black pepper to taste

Fresh or rehydrated dried seaweed, optional

Lemon wedges to garnish

Note: Silicone cupcake cups are perfect to hold each oyster shell to cook. You can also serve them with oyster shells in them for balance, instead of using the customary rock salt, crushed ice or seaweed.

Shuck the oysters. Take out the meat and put the meat and the liquid into a bowl. Rinse them in their liquid to eliminate any pieces of shell and gritty debris and put the cleaned oysters in a separate bowl. Save the oyster liquid for later. Refrigerate the oysters until ready to use. Discard the top shells. Wash the bottom shells, place them in silicone cupcake cups and set aside.

In a skillet, melt the ghee over medium heat. Add the bacon and cook until crispy, for about 5 to 8 minutes. Remove ½ of the bacon to a paper towel–lined plate and set aside to use as a topping. Add the chopped onion to the skillet and cook for about 5 minutes, or until the onion is soft. Add the garlic and cook for about 3 minutes, until soft but not burnt. Add the spring greens and fresh parsley to the skillet and stir for about 2 minutes, until the greens are wilted. Add the almond flour to the skillet and mix all the ingredients until everything is incorporated well. Add salt and pepper to taste. Set the green mixture aside to cool.

Take out the oysters from the refrigerator and place them in the shells while they are resting in the silicone cupcake cups. Preheat the air fryer to 390°F (200°C).

Spoon about a tablespoon (9 g) of the green mixture on top of each oyster. Repeat until all the oyster shells are filled. Carefully place 4 cupcake cups with oyster shells inside the basket. Set the timer for 5 minutes. When the timer goes off, carefully take them out and put them onto a platter. Repeat with the remaining oysters. When they are done, sprinkle the bacon bits, reserved chopped onions and fresh parsley on top. If using, place the fresh seaweed on the serving plate. Take the oyster shells out of the cupcake cups and nestle them into the seaweed to balance the shells in their place. Squeeze lemon juice and the oyster liquid over the oysters before serving.

Stuffed PORTOBELLO MUSHROOMS

These stuffed mushrooms are not your mama's mushrooms. They are filled with salty sea air from the fresh clams and a hint of sweetness from the coconut flour. The Italian herb seasoning makes this classic appetizer quick to mix and bake in the air fryer. You can make the stuffing ahead of time and assemble the mushrooms right before putting them in the air fryer.

COOK TIME: 10 MINUTES + 9 MINUTES STOVETOP COOKING || SERVINGS: 6

¼ cup + 1 tbsp (75 ml) extra-virgin olive oil (EVOO), divided

¼ cup (38 g) chopped onion

½ cup (75 g) finely chopped carrots

2 cloves garlic, minced

¼ cup (45 g) chopped clams

¼ cup (10 g) chopped fresh parsley, divided (reserve 2 tbsp for garnish)

2 tbsp (12 g) coconut flour

Pinch of sea salt

Black pepper, to taste

1 large egg, beaten

1 tbsp (6 g) tapioca flour

½ tsp Italian seasoning (page 52)

6 medium portobello mushrooms, 2–3" (5–7.6 cm) diameter each

Horseradish Ranch Dipping Sauce (page 192)

For the filling, heat a small frying pan over medium heat. Add 1 tablespoon (15 ml) of EVOO and sauté the onion for 5 minutes, until soft. Add the carrots, garlic and clams and cook for 2 minutes. Add 2 tablespoons (5 g) of parsley, coconut flour, salt and pepper and stir for 2 minutes, or until the carrots are soft. Turn off the heat and let the mixture cool. Transfer the mixture to a mixing bowl and add the beaten egg, tapioca and Italian seasoning, and mix well. Set aside.

Using a dry kitchen towel or paper towel, wipe the outside of the mushroom caps. Take the stems out and discard. Wipe the inside of the caps and set them on a platter. Scoop about 1 to 2 tablespoons (10 to 20 g) of the mixture into the caps to stuff them and set aside.

Preheat the air fryer to 360°F (180°C).

Add the remaining oil to an oil spritzer and spray the basket. Place the stuffed mushrooms in the basket and spray the top of the mushrooms as well. Close the basket and set the timer for 10 minutes.

When the timer goes off, carefully take the mushrooms out and place onto a platter. Garnish with the remaining parsley and serve immediately with Horseradish Ranch Dipping Sauce.

Note: An oil spritzer is a convenient and inexpensive tool to spray the basket with oil so foods don't stick. You can also spray the food before frying to make them crispy. Fill it with either extra-virgin olive oil or avocado oil and use liberally.

WONTON Bites

If you ask me, the best part about wontons or dumplings is not the skin but the meat stuffing. So why bother making the wraps when what you really want is the inside? This recipe is quick to mix and fry in the air fryer, so you don't have to bother with hot oil or steamers. Just pop these gingery minced pork balls in the basket, and 10 minutes later you'll have fun appetizers ready to please the crowd. The simple ginger dipping sauce makes these bites even more special. Make the sauce in advance so you can serve it with the piping hot wonton bites immediately.

COOK TIME: 10 MINUTES || SERVINGS: 4

---

1 lb (450 g) ground pork

1 tsp grated fresh ginger

2 cloves garlic, minced

½ tsp white pepper

2 tsp (10 ml) coconut aminos

2 tbsp (12 g) tapioca flour

¼ cup (12 g) chopped chives

¼ cup (10 g) finely chopped fresh cilantro, reserve some for garnish

Ginger Dipping Sauce (page 188)

Combine all the ingredients except the dipping sauce in a medium-sized bowl and mix well. Take about 1 to 2 tablespoons (10 to 20 g) of the mixture and make into small, bite-sized balls.

Preheat the air fryer to 360°F (180°C).

Place the bite-sized balls in the basket, as many as you can fit. You should be able to fit all of them in the basket. Close the basket and set the timer for 10 minutes. When the timer goes off, place the wonton bites on a plate, garnish with cilantro and serve with Ginger Dipping Sauce.

Kimchi DEVILED EGGS

Who would think to add kimchi to deviled eggs besides this Korean cook? Regardless of whether you are Korean or not, make this classic recipe with a gut-healthy twist. You could either cringe at the thought of biting into a spicy egg yolk mixture or you can moan with delight as you chow down on these salty, spicy, savory bites. I think the choice is clear.

COOK TIME: 11 MINUTES ‖ SERVINGS: 4

8 hard-boiled eggs, cooked using your favorite method or in the air fryer (Eggs Three Ways, page 167)

3 tbsp (65 g) finely chopped ripe kimchi

3 tsp (15 ml) Homemade Mayo (page 180)

2 strips of crispy bacon, finely chopped (Baconomics, page 168), for garnish

2 tbsp (6 g) finely chopped fresh scallions, for garnish

Preheat the air fryer to 300°F (150°C) and make the hard-boiled eggs according to the recipe on page 167.

Peel the hard-boiled eggs and cut them in half. Take out the yolks and place them in a mixing bowl. Place the egg whites on a platter and set aside.

Pick out the soft, leafy parts of the kimchi, place them in your hand and squeeze out the liquid and set aside. In a food processor, add the egg yolks, kimchi and mayo and pulse a few times until they are blended well but not pureed.

Fill the egg white halves liberally with the yolk and kimchi mixture. Garnish with the bacon and scallions before serving.

Note: "Ripe" kimchi is kimchi that is not just made (fresh), but is a few days old.

FOR BREAKING YOUR FASTS

I don't have to tell you how important breakfast is. And when you are running late in the morning—you know who you are—having a nourishing meal is the last thing on your mind. I get it. I don't have to commute to work and I sometimes forget to eat breakfast, too. So I started batch-cooking foods like Spinach Frittata (page 25), Quick-Bake Granola (page 26) and Quick and Easy Breakfast Sausage Cups (page 29) and freezing them. When I need a quick meal, I pop them in the air fryer to reheat and I'm set for the day. If I have more time to cook breakfast in the morning, Huevos Rancheros (page 22) wins every time. I love the warm tomato sauce with eggs over easy on crispy tostadas, and it's so easy to make in the air fryer! Oh, and how can I forget one of my favorite comfort breakfasts, Healthy Biscuits and Gravy (page 33). The texture of the biscuits is light, and it tastes like the authentic southern-style biscuit but made in the air fryer. I hope you try it because I know it'll become one of your favorite breakfasts. Start your day right with quick and easy foods that you make or reheat in the air fryer in a jiffy.

Huevos RANCHEROS

This classic Latin American breakfast is simple but oh so delicioso! Serve up soft eggs on top of warmed tomatoes and a crispy tostada, and you're set to conquer the day! Crispy Tostadas made in the air fryer make it easy to plan, so make them ahead of time and assemble this nourishing platter as the coffee maker does its magic.

COOK TIME: 12 MINUTES + 5–7 MINUTES STOVETOP COOKING || SERVINGS: 2

2 tbsp (30 ml) avocado oil

1 cup (150 g) chopped onion

2 tsp (6 g) chopped garlic (about 2 cloves)

2 cups (320 g) chopped tomatoes

1 tbsp + 1 tsp (3 g) chopped fresh cilantro, divided

2 Tostadas (page 176)

4 large eggs

2 tbsp (8 g) cooked bacon bits, optional (Baconomics, page 168)

2 avocados, peeled and sliced

Pinch of black sesame seeds

Heat the avocado oil in a small saucepan on medium heat. Add the onion, garlic and tomatoes and cook for 5 to 7 minutes, until the onion is soft and the tomatoes are cooked. Add 1 tablespoon (2 g) of cilantro, stir and set the mixture aside.

Place 2 ovenproof skillets or deep dishes in the air fryer basket and preheat to 360°F (180°C).

When the air fryer reaches the desired temperature, carefully take out the skillet or the dish, set on a trivet and place the tostadas in the bottom of each skillet. Divide the warm tomato mixture in half, and add on top of each tostada. Create a crater in the middle for the eggs.

Crack two eggs in a small bowl and carefully transfer them to the middle of the crater in the skillet without breaking the yolks. Repeat with the second skillet. Add the bacon bits, if using, on top of the egg yolks in each tostada and place one skillet in the basket. Set the second skillet aside. Put the timer on for 6 minutes. When the timer goes off, carefully take out the skillet and loosely cover to keep warm. Cook the second skillet for 6 minutes. When the second skillet is done, add the avocado slices and the remaining cilantro to each tostada, sprinkle with black sesame seeds and serve immediately.

Spinach FRITTATA

My husband and I were arguing about whether to call this dish a quiche or frittata. For the record, this is a frittata because it's a crustless quiche. See how he could be easily confused here? Regardless of what he calls this dish, he loves it. It's nutritious and easy to make in the air fryer. But most of all, it's delicious!

COOK TIME: 12 MINUTES ‖ SERVINGS: 2

4 large eggs

1 cup (150 g) chopped spinach

¼ cup (50 g) chopped bell pepper

¼ cup (60 g) chopped shallots

1 tbsp (2 g) chopped fresh parsley

¼ tsp curry powder

¼ tsp sea salt

¼ tsp black pepper

In a medium-sized mixing bowl, beat the four eggs. Then add the rest of the ingredients and mix well.

Place an ovenproof skillet or deep dish in the basket of the air fryer and preheat the air fryer to 360°F (180°C).

When the desired temperature is reached, carefully take out the hot skillet or dish and place onto a trivet. Transfer the quiche mixture to the skillet or the dish, then place it in the fryer basket and set the timer for 12 minutes. Close the basket and bake until the timer goes off or until a toothpick comes out clean when inserted. Serve immediately.

Quick-Bake GRANOLA

Being on the Paleo diet doesn't mean you can't have easy or quick breakfasts like granola. This grain-free granola is baked in the air fryer with nutritionally dense ingredients. It's naturally sweetened with dates and uses soaked nuts. Don't like the nuts listed? Use your favorites. Pecans, Brazilian and even macadamia nuts work well. Bake this in advance, store in an airtight container and have it handy for mornings when you can't cook!

COOK TIME: 12 MINUTES || MAKES: 3 CUPS (270 G)

20 Medjool dates

½ cup (85 g) almonds or walnuts, soaked overnight

½ cup (85 g) cashews, soaked overnight

½ cup (40 g) shredded coconut

½ cup (80 g) hemp seeds

½ cup (75 g) raisins

½ tsp ground cinnamon

1 tsp vanilla extract

In a food processor, add the dates, almonds and cashews, and pulse a few times until the mixture is coarsely chopped. Add the shredded coconut and hemp seeds and pulse a couple of times until they are thoroughly incorporated. Transfer the mixture to a large bowl. Add the raisins, cinnamon and vanilla and mix well.

Line an ovenproof skillet or deep dish with parchment paper. Preheat the air fryer to 360°F (180°C).

Transfer half of the granola mixture to the skillet or deep dish, and spread evenly. Place the skillet in the basket and bake the mixture for 6 minutes, or until slightly brown but not burnt. Mix the granola halfway through. When the timer goes off, move it to a bowl and transfer the remaining granola mixture to the skillet. Bake for 6 minutes and mix the granola halfway through. When the timer goes off, transfer the granola to the bowl with the first batch, mix them together and let it cool.

You can serve with your favorite dairy-free milk and store the remaining granola in an air-tight glass container. Use within one week if stored at room temperature or up to two weeks in the refrigerator.

Quick AND EASY BREAKFAST SAUSAGE CUPS

These breakfast sausage cups are so easy to make in the air fryer. They are quick to assemble and will be done even before your morning coffee is ready. You could also make a huge batch and freeze them to reheat in the air fryer for busy mornings when you are pressed for time. Can't get easier than that. I'm all for simple mornings, aren't you?

COOK TIME: 15 MINUTES || SERVINGS: 8

4 large eggs

1 cup (200 g) sweet potatoes, chopped into small cubes

½ cup (75 g) diced onions

3 tsp (2 g) chopped fresh parsley (reserve 1 tsp for garnish), or 1 tsp dried parsley

2 cups (280 g) cooked Ground Breakfast Sausage (page 175)

In a large bowl, crack the eggs and beat with a whisk. Add the sweet potatoes, onions, parsley and sausage and mix well.

Preheat the air fryer to 360°F (180°C).

Transfer the mixture into a large measuring cup to pour easily. Pour even amounts of the mixture into 8 silicone cupcake cups. You can either bring the air fryer basket near the cupcake cups and carefully place each cup in the basket or, if you have a steady hand, you can place the empty cups in the basket and pour in the mixture.

Set the timer for 15 minutes. Check the cups halfway through baking to make sure they are not getting too brown or burning. When the timer goes off, carefully take out the cups—they will be hot and less wobbly—and serve immediately. These nutrient-dense all-in-one sausage cups are great for breakfast or for lunch with spring greens on the side! They freeze well, so make extra batches and reheat as breakfast on-the-go for those busy mornings.

Sweet POTATO HASH WITH OVER-EASY EGGS

My daughter loves making this sweet potato hash in the air fryer. She makes double batches to share with her brother since he will undoubtedly ask her to share. Since they can't have eggs, she makes the hash without eggs but with extra bacon and it still tastes delicious. Me? I love the runny yolk from the over-easy eggs, so I cook the eggs right on top of the hash. Easy peasy. Nourishing breakfasts rock!

COOK TIME: 18 MINUTES ‖ SERVINGS: 2

2 cups (400 g) diced sweet potatoes, cut into ½" (13-mm) cubes

1 cup (150 g) chopped onion

6 strips bacon, chopped

2 tsp (10 g) garlic powder

1 tbsp (2 g) chopped fresh parsley, or 1 tsp dried parsley

¼ tsp paprika

4 large eggs

Pinch of black sesame seeds, for topping

Combine all the ingredients, except the eggs and sesame seeds, in a bowl and mix well.

Place an ovenproof dish or skillet in the air fryer basket and preheat to 360°F (180°C).

When the desired temperature is reached, carefully put the skillet or dish onto a trivet and place the sweet potato hash mixture in the preheated dish or skillet.

Set the timer for 10 minutes. When the timer goes off, open the basket and mix the hash. Create a crater in the middle and crack the eggs inside the crater. Set the timer for 8 minutes and bake until the timer goes off. Take the dish or skillet out, divide the hash mixture and eggs onto two plates, sprinkle with black sesame seeds and serve immediately.

Healthy BISCUITS AND GRAVY

This is such a quintessential Southern breakfast. Make the biscuits in the air fryer and make the homemade Ground Breakfast Sausage in advance. And when you are in the mood for this Southern comfort, drench them in creamy, savory gravy for a happy-belly breakfast.

COOK TIME: 12 MINUTES + 5 MINUTES STOVETOP COOKING || SERVINGS: 4

BISCUITS

½ cup (50 g) coconut flour

1 cup (95 g) extra fine blanched almond flour

¼ cup (25 g) tapioca flour

½ tsp baking soda

⅛ tsp sea salt

¾ cup (175 ml) full-fat coconut milk yogurt

2 tbsp (30 ml) ghee, at room temperature

1 tbsp (15 ml) raw honey

2 tsp (10 ml) vanilla extract

½ tsp apple cider vinegar

SAUSAGE AND GRAVY

⅓ cup (30 g) cassava flour (I use Otto's Cassava Flour)

2 cups (475 ml) *cold* bone broth

Salt, to taste

1 lb (450 g) cooked Ground Breakfast Sausage (page 175)

2 tsp (2 g) chopped fresh parsley, for garnish

Pinch of black pepper

For the biscuits, combine the dry ingredients in a medium-sized mixing bowl and sift. In a small mixing bowl, combine the yogurt, ghee, honey, vanilla extract and apple cider vinegar and mix well.

Preheat the air fryer to 360°F (180°C).

Add the wet ingredients to the dry ingredients and mix until a dough forms. Do not knead too much. Otherwise, the biscuits will be hard. Divide the dough into 4 balls. Form the shape of a biscuit about 1 inch (2.5 cm) thick. When the air fryer is ready, place the dough in the basket. Set the timer for 12 minutes. Check at 10 minutes to make sure they are browned but not burnt.

Meanwhile, make the sausage and gravy. Whisk the cassava flour with the bone broth in a small saucepan. When they are thoroughly mixed, bring the mixture to a boil over medium heat. Lower the temperature, add salt and the cooked ground sausage and simmer for 5 minutes while stirring constantly, until the gravy thickens.

Place the biscuits on a plate and pour the sausage and gravy mixture on top. Sprinkle on chopped parsley and black pepper and serve immediately.

MIDDAY ENERGIZERS

You know what's the worst? Getting the munchies in the middle of the day. You just had lunch a little while ago and dinner is only a few hours away, so you don't want to overindulge, but you need something to curb your hunger pangs until dinner. Maybe they're not really "hunger pangs," but just weakness to food? Regardless, you want to grab a snack that's not sugary junk. I got just the things for ya. Nosh on these guilt-free, nourishing snacks so you don't run to the nearest vending machine only to regret it later.

Some may even seem like a meal, like Savory Sweet Potato Stacks (page 36), Paleo Falafel Platter (page 39) and Meatloaf Sliders (page 40). But the Chewy Gooey Energy Snack Balls (page 43) are just enough to give you a burst of energy to squish those mid-afternoon hunger pangs. I'm not responsible for what you would do with that burst of energy, but I assume it'll be for something good.

Savory SWEET POTATO STACKS

Sweet potato slices make great snacks all on their own, but when you use them as a base to layer savory ingredients on top, you've just promoted them to a whole 'nother level. I'm using Lemon Thyme Chicken Breasts in this recipe because the seasoning is subtle and does not overpower the sweet potatoes. Pile some fresh vegetables a mile high, drizzle balsamic glaze for the tartness and sweetness, and now you have the tastiest midday snack in the office.

COOK TIME: 20 MINUTES ‖ SERVINGS: 4 (8 SLICES)

2 large (12–15 oz [340–425 g]) sweet potatoes

2 tbsp extra-virgin olive oil (EVOO), for coating

2 cooked Lemon Thyme Chicken Breasts (page 83), or plain chicken breasts

¼ cup (60 ml) balsamic glaze, divided

2 apples, sliced

¼ cup (50 g) sliced, blanched almonds

2 cups (80 g) arugula

1 cup (150 g) sliced sun-dried tomatoes

1 cup (150 g) sliced roasted peppers

Wash the sweet potatoes, making sure to get all the debris out of the eyes of the potatoes. You can either peel the skin or leave it on. Carefully cut a small thin slice along the side of the sweet potatoes, lay that side flat on the cutting board, and continue to slice them into ⅛-inch (3-mm)-thick slices. You should have about 3 to 4 long slices from one potato, a total of 6 to 8 slices. Brush EVOO on both sides of each slice.

Preheat the air fryer to 360°F (180°C).

When the desired temperature is reached, place as many sweet potato slices in the basket as you can, and set the timer for 15 minutes. Cook until the timer goes off. Repeat until all the slices are cooked.

Meanwhile, slice the cooked chicken breasts across the grain of the meat. Take the sweet potato slices out of the basket and put them on a platter. Brush one side of the sweet potato slices with balsamic glaze. Then place the chicken breast slices on top, put the slices back in the basket and cook for 5 minutes. When the timer goes off, take them back to the platter and stack on slices of apple, almonds, arugula, sun-dried tomatoes, roasted peppers and drizzle with more balsamic glaze. Serve immediately.

Paleo FALAFEL PLATTER

My farmers' market has a falafel stand and the smell of deep-frying falafel always makes me hungry. Since authentic falafels are made with chickpeas, I wanted to re-create this Middle Eastern dish with Paleo-friendly ingredients without deep-frying. I'm using soaked cashews in this recipe, but almonds would be just as tasty. Serve with a side of chopped salad and tahini dressing and you'll be transported to the outdoor market in Egypt.

COOK TIME: 15–20 MINUTES || SERVINGS: 4

FALAFEL

1 cup (150 g) unsalted raw cashews, soaked overnight

4 tbsp (25 g) extra fine blanched almond flour

1 tbsp (5 g) coconut flour

1 tbsp (5 g) arrowroot flour

1 large egg white

2 tbsp (5 g) chopped fresh cilantro

2 tbsp (5 g) chopped fresh parsley

4 cloves garlic

1 cup (150 g) chopped onion

1 tsp sea salt

1 tsp cumin

CHOPPED SALAD

1 cup (160 g) diced tomato

1 cup (150 g) diced cucumber

1 cup (110 g) diced green bell pepper

TAHINI DRESSING

⅓ cup (55 g) toasted sesame seeds

2 tbsp (30 ml) extra-virgin olive oil (EVOO)

1 tsp garlic powder

1 tsp lemon juice

3–4 tbsp (45–60 ml) warm water

A pinch of sea salt

In a food processor, add all the ingredients for the falafel and pulse a few times, but do not puree. Otherwise, you'll end up with dense flour balls. You want some pieces of cashew in the bite. When done with the pulsing, refrigerate the mixture for at least 2 hours. I take the blade out of the food processor and refrigerate the pitcher. No need to transfer the mixture to another bowl for you to wash. Call me lazy.

When you're ready to make the falafel, preheat the air fryer to 360°F (180°C).

Meanwhile, add the vegetables for the salad to a medium-sized mixing bowl and refrigerate. Make the tahini dressing by pureeing the toasted sesame seeds with EVOO. When the consistency is like peanut butter, add the garlic powder and lemon juice and slowly drizzle with warm water until the consistency is more like Caesar salad dressing. Add a pinch of sea salt and set aside.

Take out the falafel mixture from the refrigerator. Using an ice cream scooper or a large serving spoon (about the size of ¼ cup [50 g]), scoop out the falafel mixture and shape them into balls. When the air fryer's desired temperature is reached, place the falafel balls in the basket, and set the timer for 15 to 20 minutes. Depending on how big the balls are, cook until the timer goes off or they are golden brown.

Serve on a bed of salad with tahini dressing.

MEATLOAF

Traditionally, meatloaf is baked and not fried. But it turns out baking slider-sized meatloaf patties for midday snacking is perfect! It's quick, and they are very moist. These mini sliders are perfect on Paleo buns of your choice, on lettuce wraps or with a side salad! They are perfect on Paleo Biscuits (page 164), too.

COOK TIME: 10 MINUTES || SERVINGS: 8–10

1 lb (450 g) ground beef (80/20 fat)

2 large eggs, beaten

¼ cup (50 g) finely chopped onion

1 clove garlic, minced

½ cup (50 g) extra fine blanched almond flour

¼ cup (25 g) coconut flour

¼ cup (60 g) ketchup

½ tsp sea salt

½ tsp black pepper

1 tbsp (15 ml) gluten-free Worcestershire sauce

1 tsp Italian seasoning (page 52)

½ tsp dried tarragon

In a large mixing bowl, combine all the ingredients and mix well. Make patties that are about 2 inches (5 cm) in diameter and about 1 inch (2.5 cm) thick. If you want to make thicker or thinner patties, make sure all of them are similar in size, so they cook properly at the same time. Place the patties on a platter and refrigerate for 10 minutes for the flour to absorb the wet ingredients and the patties to become firm.

Preheat the air fryer to 360°F (180°C).

Place as many patties as you can fit in the basket and close. Set the timer for 10 minutes. Check the patties halfway through. When the timer goes off, take them out, place on a serving platter and cover until all the patties are cooked.

Chewy GOOEY ENERGY SNACK BALLS

How many times have you bought snack bars and they didn't taste as good as you expected? These snack balls are nutritionally dense, they're naturally sweetened with dates and you can use whatever nuts you like so you won't be disappointed! You can store them in airtight containers or freeze them and you'll never have to buy another energy bar again!

COOK TIME: 6 MINUTES || SERVINGS: 12

¼ cup (35 g) chia seeds

½ cup (120 ml) water

1 cup (150 g) nuts of your choice (almonds, walnuts, pecans or combination), soaked overnight

20 Medjool dates

½ cup (40 g) coconut flakes or shredded coconut

½ cup (80 g) hemp seeds

½ cup (80 g) toasted sesame seeds

1 tsp cinnamon

1 tsp vanilla extract

½ cup (140 g) chocolate cacao nibs, optional

Combine the chia seeds and water in a small bowl and set aside for 30 minutes. Meanwhile, pulse the nuts and dates in a food processor until they are coarsely chopped. When they are pressed together between your fingers, the mixture should stick together. Add the coconut flakes, hemp seeds, sesame seeds and soaked chia seeds to the nuts mixture. Pulse a couple of times until they are mixed in. Transfer the mixture to a bowl and add the rest of the ingredients. Mold the mixture into small-sized balls about 1 inch (2.5 cm) in diameter.

Preheat the air fryer to 360°F (180°C).

Place as many balls in the basket as can fit and set the timer for 6 minutes. When the timer goes off, take the balls out and place onto a platter. Bake the rest of the balls until all of them are done. You can store these energy balls in an airtight container and refrigerate for up to two weeks.

Savory ALMOND CRACKERS

I should have named these "Emily Crackers" because my daughter loves them, and she doesn't even like regular crackers. These are savory and the almond flour makes them a bit sweet. They are addicting and nourishing at the same time. Can you ask for a better snack?

COOK TIME: 8 MINUTES || MAKES: ½ POUND (230 G)

1 cup (100 g) extra fine blanched almond flour

1 cup (100 g) tapioca flour

¼ tsp sea salt

¼ tsp curry powder

¼ tsp cumin

½ tsp garlic powder

½ cup (120 ml) coconut cream, full fat

1 tbsp (15 ml) extra-virgin olive oil (EVOO)

1 tbsp (10 g) Italian seasoning (page 52)

Combine all the ingredients in a medium-sized mixing bowl. Mix the ingredients to form a dough. Place the dough between 2 pieces of parchment paper and roll out with a rolling pin until it's ¼ inch (6 mm) thick. Carefully, tear the dough apart into irregular pieces big enough to handle, about the size of your palm. The smaller the pieces, the crispier the edges will get. Place the pieces in a single layer in the air fryer basket and place the rack over them. This will prevent the crackers from curling and flying around inside.

Preheat the air fryer to 360°F (180°C).

Place the basket in the air fryer and set the timer for 8 minutes. Check at 5 minutes to make sure the crackers are baking evenly. Continue to cook until the timer goes off. The crackers should be brown. If there are any white spots, put them back in the air fryer and bake for a couple of minutes more. When all of them are done, store in an airtight container for up to 2 weeks at room temperature.

Paleo CRACKERS

These crackers don't last more than a day in my house. They are salty, garlicky and so good with everything or eaten alone. They are nothing like "conventional" crackers; they are so much better. Carry them with you to lunches where they don't serve Paleo bread. Your friends will want these crackers though, so bring extra.

COOK TIME: 8 MINUTES || MAKES: ½ POUND (230 G)

CRACKERS

½ cup (50 g) cassava flour (I use Otto's Cassava Flour)

¼ cup (25 g) tapioca flour

2 tbsp (10 g) coconut flour

2 tbsp (25 g) coconut sugar

½ tsp baking soda

½ tsp sea salt

½ cup (120 ml) coconut cream, full fat

¼ cup (60 ml) melted ghee

¼ tsp extra-virgin olive oil (EVOO)

1 tsp garlic powder

2 tsp (5 g) Italian seasoning (page 52)

GARLIC AND HERB OIL

2 tbsp (30 ml) extra-virgin olive oil (EVOO)

2 tsp (5 g) Italian seasoning (page 52)

1 tsp garlic powder

1 clove garlic, minced

Combine all the crackers ingredients in a medium-sized mixing bowl. Mix the ingredients to form a dough. Place the dough between pieces of parchment paper and roll with a rolling pin until it's ¼ inch (6 mm) thick. Carefully, tear the dough apart into irregular pieces big enough to handle, about the size of your palm. The smaller the pieces, the crispier the edges will get. Place the pieces in a single layer in the basket and place the rack over them. This will prevent the crackers from curling and flying around inside.

Preheat the air fryer to 360°F (180°C).

Place the basket in the air fryer and set the timer for 8 minutes. Check at 5 minutes to make sure the crackers are baking evenly. Continue to cook until the timer goes off. The crackers should be brown. If there are any white areas, put them back in the air fryer and bake a couple of minutes more. While they are baking, mix the ingredients for the garlic and herb oil in a small bowl. When all of the crackers are done, brush them with the garlic and herb oil. Store them in an airtight container at room temperature for up to 2 weeks.

MOOVERS & GRAZERS

Many of the recipes in this section are my family's favorites. We love tender meats like filet mignon and rib eye steaks, so the first recipe I wanted to share with you had to be the first beef meal I had after I stopped being a vegan, Filet Mignon with Herbs and Roasted Garlic (page 52). And you might be wondering, "You want me to cook the most expensive piece of meat, filet mignon, in an air fryer?" Ya betcha! You will love how easy it is without sacrificing flavor. And my family's favorite Korean LA-Style Short Ribs (Kalbi) (page 56) will be your family's favorite, too! These ribs cook fast in the air fryer, and it's oh-so-finger-licking good! And another family favorite—the ONLY way my family eats lamb—Lazy Lamb Chops (page 55)! And an air fryer cookbook can't be written without mentioning the good ole Healthy Chicken-Fried Steak (page 68) from the South, which has no chicken in it! Go figure.

I hope you enjoy these dishes that will not only satisfy your taste buds but also the dishwashers on duty since there will be no grease splattered on the stovetop or counters from frying fatty proteins.

Roasted BRUSSELS SPROUTS WITH BACON

Brussels sprouts get a bad rap with some people, but with bacon mixed in, these sprouts will be the first to be gone from the dinner table. Use the air fryer to roast and brown the outside faster. When cooked with uncured bacon without sulfites, this healthy version will make even the skeptics in your family love them!

COOK TIME: 15 MINUTES || SERVINGS: 2

1 lb (450 g) fresh brussels sprouts

½ tsp sea salt

½ tsp ground black pepper

1 tsp garlic powder

1 tbsp (10 g) blanched almond slivers

1 tbsp (15 ml) extra-virgin olive oil (EVOO)

2 strips uncured bacon

2 tbsp (5 g) chopped fresh scallions, for garnish

Wash the brussels sprouts and cut them in half. Put them in a large mixing bowl, add the rest of the ingredients, except the bacon and scallions, and mix well.

Preheat the air fryer to 390°F (200°C).

Put the mixture in the air fryer basket. Cut the bacon into 1-inch (2.5-cm) pieces and put them on top of the brussels sprouts. Close the basket.

When the desired temperature is reached, set the timer for 15 minutes. At 7 minutes, use tongs to mix the brussels sprouts and bacon around in the basket. Place the basket back in the air fryer and continue to cook until the timer goes off. Check to see if the bacon pieces are done and the brussels sprouts are soft. When they are cooked, put them in a bowl, sprinkle with scallions and serve immediately.

Filet MIGNON WITH HERBS AND ROASTED GARLIC

I know what you're thinking. Why would I take a chance with cooking one of the most expensive cuts of meat in an air fryer? Believe me, I thought the same thing, too. But this lean cut of beef is perfect for the air fryer because it cooks very quickly and keeps in the moisture, making it very juicy and tender inside. Smear some roasted garlic on the outside and it will not disappoint!

COOK TIME: 13 MINUTES (MEDIUM RARE) || SERVINGS: 2

2 filets mignon, similar in thickness, preferably 2–2½" (5–6 cm) thick

1 tsp Italian seasoning (see below)

2 tbsp (30 ml) extra-virgin olive oil (EVOO)

1 tsp sea salt

4 cloves Roasted Garlic, finely chopped (page 171)

ITALIAN SEASONING

1 tsp dried oregano

1 tsp dried thyme

1 tsp dried rubbed sage

1 tsp dried marjoram

1 tsp dried basil

First, bring the meat to room temperature. In a shallow dish, combine the Italian seasoning, EVOO, salt and roasted garlic. Coat the filets on both sides and all around. Massage the herb mixture well into the meat with your hands, then loosely cover it and set aside for 30 minutes.

Place an ovenproof skillet or deep dish in the air fryer basket and preheat to 390°F (200°C).

When the air fryer is ready, open the basket carefully, and place both filets on the preheated skillet or deep dish. Close the basket and set the timer for 13 minutes. At 8 minutes, open the basket and turn the meat over. Close the basket. When the timer goes off, open the basket, and spoon the herbs and fat dripping from the dish on top of the meat. Close the basket again and let the meat rest until you are ready to serve with your favorite sides. This recipe is for medium rare with an internal temperature of 130°F (55°C). If you like it medium, cook 2 to 3 minutes more until the internal temperature is 145°F (65°C). If you like it well done, wait until the internal temperature is 155°F (70°C). Always use a meat thermometer to check the temperature.

Note: You can fry filet mignon directly in the basket, but the fat drippings will likely make the air fryer smoke. Also, using a heat resistant deep dish or a cast-iron skillet will help the meat retain the flavor better and be more tender. So, I highly recommend using an ovenproof deep dish or cast-iron skillet, which is my favorite vessel for cooking filet mignon.

 Lazy LAMB CHOPS

When I was on the sidelines waiting with other moms for our children's games to finish, do you know what our biggest worries were? Figuring out what to cook for dinner and how fast we could cook once we made our mad dash home. One of the moms shared this simple, yet flavorful recipe one summer, and I couldn't thank her enough. I made these lamb chops almost every week on the grill, and my family, who hated lamb chops before, couldn't get enough of them! Unfortunately, we couldn't grill in the winter, so we really missed having them when the weather got colder.

Enter the air fryer. Oh boy. Air fryers can make these lamb chops so tender without charring, and now we enjoy this simple and quick protein meal even in the winter. This is the only way my family eats lamb chops!

COOK TIME: 12 MINUTES (MEDIUM RARE) ‖ SERVINGS: 2

---

2 tbsp (30 ml) avocado oil or high-quality extra-virgin olive oil (EVOO)

¼ cup (60 ml) Paleo Dijon mustard

¼ cup (60 ml) gluten-free Worcestershire sauce

½ tsp salt

½ tsp black pepper

8 Australian lamb chops

Chopped fresh chives or mint, for garnish

To make the marinade, combine the oil, mustard, Worcestershire, salt and pepper in a bowl and stir until combined.

On a large platter or a glass baking dish, place the lamb chops in one layer and marinate in the marinade for about 30 minutes or overnight, turning them over once.

Preheat the air fryer to 390°F (200°C).

When the temperature reaches 390°F (200°C), take the lamb chops from the platter and gently shake off any excess marinade. Place 4 lamb chops in the basket in one layer, leaving some spaces in between. Set the timer for 12 minutes. At about 6 minutes, turn the lamb chops over and continue to cook until the timer goes off and the outside is brown but not burnt. Repeat with the remaining lamb chops. Cover the cooked lamb chops until the last batch is done. When the timer goes off, take the lamb chops out, garnish with chopped chives or mint and serve immediately.

Note: This recipe's time is for medium rare, which is very tender and slightly pink but no running redness inside. If you like well done, cook for 14 minutes. If you prefer rare, cook for 10 minutes. Keep in mind, every air fryer is different so check for doneness by using a meat thermometer.

Korean LA-STYLE SHORT RIBS (KALBI)

Normally, I grill *kalbi* on the outdoor BBQ grill and my neighbors always wonder what smells so good. Well, when you make this kalbi in the air fryer, your family will run to the kitchen, wondering the same. This is a Paleorized version of the classic Korean BBQ beef recipe, using liquid aminos instead of soy sauce and honey instead of white sugar. And I bet your family will gobble them up even before you can take them out of the fryer! Just make sure to have plenty of napkins handy because they'll want to use their fingers to dig in. Don't blame me for dirty sleeves.

COOK TIME: 12 MINUTES || SERVINGS: 4

½ cup (120 ml) coconut aminos

¼ cup (60 ml) raw honey (more if you want it sweeter)

1 small apple, skinned, cored and pureed

1 tsp blackstrap molasses

5 cloves garlic, minced

½ tsp minced fresh ginger

¼ cup (10 g) chopped fresh scallions

2 tbsp (20 g) toasted sesame seeds, plus more for garnish

1 tbsp (15 g) black pepper

1 tsp sesame oil

8 LA-style short ribs (short ribs cut across the bones)

Fresh scallions, cut diagonally, for garnish

Lemon wedges, as garnish and to squeeze juice on top

Lettuce leaves, optional, to be used as wraps

Cauli Couscous, optional, for serving (page 172)

You can make the marinade in advance and marinate the ribs for at least 30 minutes. To make the marinade, combine the aminos, honey, apple puree, molasses, garlic, ginger, scallions, sesame seeds, pepper and oil in a bowl and mix well.

Preheat the air fryer to 390°F (200°C).

If you didn't marinate the meat in advance, brush the ribs with the marinade while waiting for the air fryer to preheat. Place 4 pieces of meat in the basket and set the timer for 12 minutes. At about 6 minutes, turn the meat over and continue to cook until the timer goes off or until brown. Take the cooked meat out, place them onto a plate and put the remaining meat in the air fryer. When the last batch is cooked, take them out and add them to the plate. Sprinkle on scallions and sesame seeds to garnish. Squeeze lemon juice on top and serve immediately. If you'd like, you can serve in lettuce wraps or with Cauli Couscous (page 172).

Beef EMPANADAS

Traditional empanadas are deep-fried and not baked. Ask a Spanish grandma and she won't accept oven-baked empanadas as empanadas. But if using a pot full of hot oil to deep-fry crispy dough filled with savory beef keeps you from making them, then the air fryer is your solution. After trying this method, you will have to make them every week because your family will demand them! You can add jalapeños for some heat or you can leave them out. You can also use pork or chicken as protein, too.

COOK TIME: 8–10 MINUTES + 10 MINUTES STOVETOP COOKING || MAKES: 8 EMPANADAS

FILLING

2 tbsp (30 ml) extra-virgin olive oil (EVOO)

1 cup (150 g) diced onion

1½ tsp (5 g) minced garlic

½ cup (55 g) diced green bell pepper

1 tsp cumin

½ lb (226 g) ground beef

1 tsp dried oregano

1 tbsp (2 g) fresh chopped cilantro

1 jalapeño pepper, diced, optional

EMPANADA CRUST

½ cup (50 g) arrowroot flour

½ cup (50 g) extra fine blanched almond flour

¼ tsp sea salt

¼ tsp cumin

¼ tsp turmeric

1 large egg, beaten

1 large egg white (for brushing the outside)

For the filling, heat the EVOO in a skillet over medium heat. Add the onion, garlic, bell pepper and cumin and sauté for about 5 minutes or until the onion is translucent. Add the ground beef and oregano and stir for 5 minutes, until the beef is cooked. Add the cilantro and diced jalapeño pepper, if using, turn off the heat, and transfer the mixture to a bowl, leaving the liquid that's formed in the skillet. Cover and refrigerate to chill for at least 30 minutes.

To make the empanada crust, combine the dry ingredients and sift. Add the beaten egg and mix well to form a dough. Set aside 2 sheets of parchment paper. Divide the dough into 8 balls. Place a ball in between the parchment papers and roll it out into a circle about ¼ inch (6 mm) thick. Repeat for the other 7 balls of dough.

Fill the dough with the filling and pinch the edges together. The thickest part should be 1 inch (2.5 cm) thick. Brush the dough with the egg white using a pastry brush. Make sure to brush all sides.

Preheat the air fryer to 360°F (180°C).

Place the empanadas in the basket and set the timer for 8 to 10 minutes. Check at 6 minutes to make sure they are browning evenly. When the timer goes off and they are brown, take them out and serve with salad, Tostones with Mojo de Ajo (page 128) or lime and cilantro cauli couscous (page 80).

SIMPLE BISON *Balls*

Bison, by nature, is a free-roaming animal that feeds on grass. If you can't find grass-fed and finished beef, bison is the next best meat to buy. I often substitute with ground bison meat from the supermarket when I run out of grass-fed ground beef from my local farm. I like to add a hint of tarragon to bison because the anise family herb adds a little more depth to the meat and hides the gamey taste of bison. These go great with zoodles.

COOK TIME: 15 MINUTES ‖ MAKES: 8 BALLS

1 lb (450 g) ground bison meat

½ cup (75 g) finely chopped onion

1 tbsp (3 g) chopped fresh parsley

½ tbsp (1 g) chopped fresh tarragon

1 tbsp (15 ml) gluten-free Worcestershire sauce

1 tsp sea salt

½ tsp black pepper

1 (12-oz [340-g]) can of your favorite marinara sauce

1 tsp chopped fresh basil, for garnish

In a large mixing bowl, place all the ingredients except the marinara sauce and basil, and mix them well. Shape the mixture into 8 balls, about 2 inches (5 cm) in diameter.

Preheat the air fryer to 360°F (180°C).

Place all the bison balls in an ovenproof deep dish or a skillet and pour the marinara sauce over them. Place the dish or the skillet in the basket and set the timer for 15 minutes. When the timer goes off and the balls are brown on the outside, take the dish or the skillet out, garnish with basil and serve immediately.

DONKATSU

Don- or *tonkatsu* is breaded and deep-fried thin pork cutlets that are very popular, not only in Japan, but worldwide. *Don* or *ton* means pork, and *katsu* means filet or thinly pounded meat. So, donkatsu is a thin pork cutlet that has been breaded and deep-fried. You can also use chicken or beef to make chicken katsu or beef katsu. Normally, donkatsu is served with hot rice and donkatsu sauce over both the meat and the rice, but if you don't eat white rice, you can eat it with Cauli Couscous (page 172).

COOK TIME: 10 MINUTES || SERVINGS: 4

4 pork tenderloins, sliced about 1"
(2.5 cm) thick

¼ tsp sea salt

½ tsp black pepper

1 cup (60 g) Breadcrumbs
(page 187), refrigerated

⅓ cup (30 g) cassava flour (I use
Otto's cassava flour)

3 large eggs, beaten

DONKATSU SAUCE

2 tbsp (30 g) ghee

½ cup (120 ml) Teriyaki Sauce
(page 183)

2 tbsp (30 ml) Paleo ketchup

4 cups (645 g) cooked white rice,
optional, for serving

Purple cabbage salad, optional,
for serving

4 cups Cauli Couscous, optional,
for serving (page 172)

Use a meat tenderizer or the back of a chef's knife to flatten out the tenderloin to about ¼ to ⅛ inch (6 to 3 mm) thick. Sprinkle each side with salt and pepper, and set aside.

Take the breadcrumbs from the refrigerator and transfer to a platter. Place the cassava flour in a shallow dish and the beaten eggs in a shallow bowl. Take the pork cutlets, dredge both sides in the cassava flour, dip them in the eggs and press each side into the breadcrumbs. Place them on a platter, cover and refrigerate for at least 30 minutes.

Preheat the air fryer to 360°F (180°C).

Place as many cutlets as you can fit in the basket of the air fryer and set the timer for 10 minutes. Check for even cooking at 5 to 6 minutes. When the timer goes off and the inside of the cutlet is opaque white and not pink when cut, place the cooked cutlets on a platter and keep them covered until all the cutlets are cooked and ready to be served.

Meanwhile, make the donkatsu sauce. In a small saucepan, melt the ghee over medium heat. Add the Teriyaki Sauce and ketchup. Whisk the sauce vigorously to emulsify the ghee into the sauce. Bring to a boil and then let it simmer while stirring for 1 to 2 minutes. Turn the heat off and set aside.

If you eat rice, scoop 1 cup (161 g) onto a plate, place the pork cutlets on top, drizzle the donkatsu sauce over the cutlets and the rice. If you don't eat rice, serve with some purple cabbage salad or Cauli Couscous (page 172).

Korean DUMPLING BOWLS (MANDU)

I remember making Korean dumplings, or *mandu*, on special holidays, like New Year's Day. Traditional Korean dumplings are made with bean sprouts, tofu and wheat dumpling wrappers, but for the Paleo version, I left them out. You can substitute steamed cabbage leaves as wrappers instead. Make the Spicy Korean Dipping Sauce (page 191) in advance and drizzle it on top before serving.

COOK TIME: 10 MINUTES + 5 MINUTES STOVETOP COOKING || MAKES: 10–12 DUMPLING BOWLS

1 head of green cabbage

1 cup (90 g) finely chopped, cooked sweet potato noodles (AKA Japchae or cellophane noodles)

1 cup (75 g) diced, fresh shiitake mushrooms

1 lb (450 g) ground pork

2 tsp (10 ml) sesame oil

1 tbsp (15 ml) coconut aminos

2 cloves garlic, minced

½ cup (75 g) chopped onion

1 tsp grated fresh ginger

1 tsp sea salt

2 tbsp (12 g) cassava flour (I like Otto's Cassava Flour)

½ cup (25 g) chopped fresh scallions

1 tsp toasted sesame seeds

Spicy Korean Dipping Sauce (page 191)

Core the cabbage around the stem with a sharp paring knife. Put about 3 cups (710 ml) of water in a stock pot, place a vegetable steamer in it and steam the cabbage for about 5 minutes until the leaves are cooked and soft but not mushy. Remove and take about 10 to 12 small cabbage leaves from the center of the cabbage to be used as "bowls." Take a few outer cabbage leaves and chop finely to yield about 1 cup (150 g). Save the rest of the cabbage to be used for dishes you may cook later.

In a large mixing bowl, combine all the ingredients, except the cabbage bowls and dipping sauce, and mix well. If the mixture is too wet, add more cassava flour until you can easily make them into balls. Refrigerate the mixture for about 20 minutes.

Preheat the air fryer to 360°F (180°C).

Take the mixture out of the refrigerator, scoop about 2 tablespoons (20 g) of the mixture and make it into a ball. Repeat until you have about 10 to 12 mandu balls. When the desired temperature is reached, place the mandu balls in the basket, and set the timer for 10 minutes.

Meanwhile, set the steamed cabbage bowls out on a platter. When the timer goes off and the balls are brown and firm, place one ball in each leaf and serve immediately with Spicy Korean Dipping Sauce.

Crispy GARLICKY PORK CHOPS

While I was growing up, I had *chuleta* with rice and beans for lunch when working in the Bronx at my family's retail business. *Chuleta* means pork chop in Spanish and they were always juicy on the inside and crispy with a garlicky oil coating on the outside. I haven't found the same type of pork chops since I left the neighborhood, but I tried to re-create them with this recipe. I tweaked the garlic oil by adding herbs, but if you want to use just garlic, the more the better. You will love it that much more.

COOK TIME: 15 MINUTES + 3–4 MINUTES STOVETOP COOKING || SERVINGS: 2

2 (1″ [2.5-cm]-thick) porterhouse pork chops (bone-in)

⅛ tsp sea salt

⅛ tsp black pepper

1–1½ cups (150–215 g) Crispy Chicharrones (page 114)

GARLIC HERB OIL

3 tbsp (45 ml) extra-virgin olive oil (EVOO)

3 cloves garlic, chopped

2 tbsp (5 g) chopped fresh parsley

2 tbsp (5 g) chopped fresh cilantro

1 tsp lime juice

Sea salt and black pepper, to taste

Note: Place the air fryer in a well-ventilated area. Because of the oil drippings from chicharrones and the pork chop, the air fryer might smoke. If it starts to smoke, take the outer basket out and drain the oil and restart the cooking process. Just remember how many more minutes you need to cook.

Sprinkle the pork chops with salt and pepper on both sides, cover and let them rest on the counter to reach room temperature. Meanwhile, put the chicharrones in a food processor and pulse a few times until the pieces are ground up, like fine breadcrumbs. One pound (454 g) of chicharrones should make about ½ cup (75 g) ground up. Transfer the chicharrones to a plate and refrigerate.

Meanwhile, make the garlic herb oil. Heat the EVOO in a small pan on medium heat and sauté the garlic for about 2 to 3 minutes, or until it is brown but not burnt. When it is done, take out the garlic pieces and set aside. Add the parsley and cilantro to the pan with the same oil and sauté for a minute. Add lime juice and a pinch of salt and pepper, stir and turn off the heat to cool. Transfer the garlic herb oil to a small bowl to serve with the pork chops later.

Take the chicharrones from the refrigerator. Coat both sides of the pork chops really well with the ground chicharrones. Press the grounds into the meat with your hands and refrigerate them for at least 15 minutes. This will allow the grounds to stick to the meat and not fly around in the air fryer.

Preheat the air fryer to 390°F (200°C). Place the pork chops in the basket and set the timer for 15 minutes.

At 13 minutes, spread the reserved garlic pieces on top of the pork chops. Close the basket and continue to cook until the timer goes off. Insert a meat thermometer in the middle of the pork chop near the bone. The desired internal temperature should be 145 to 160°F (65 to 70°C).

Serve immediately with the garlic herb oil on the side.

Healthy CHICKEN-FRIED STEAK

I never understood chicken-fried steak. The first time I heard it, I thought I'd get a fried slab of steak and a chicken filet, together. Although that sounded a bit disturbing, I ordered it for my daughter because when you are in Texas, you order what Texans eat. So, when I saw just the fried steak, I asked the waiter if they made a mistake. How embarrassing. My daughter thought it was the best thing she ate on that trip, so, of course, I had to re-create it. I'm pretty sure I made my daughter—and that laughing waiter—proud with this recipe.

COOK TIME: 12 MINUTES || SERVINGS: 4

4 sirloin steaks, or bottom round cut into steaks, 1" (2.5 cm) thick

¼ tsp sea salt

½ tsp black pepper

½ cup (50 g) cassava flour (I use Otto's Cassava Flour)

3 large eggs, beaten

1 cup (150 g) Breadcrumbs (page 187)

1 cup (235 ml) *cold* chicken stock

¼ tsp freshly ground black pepper

1 tsp chopped fresh parsley, for garnish

Feisty Sweet Potatoes, optional (page 121)

Use a meat tenderizer or the back of a chef's knife to flatten out the steaks to about ¼ to ⅛ inch (6 to 3 mm) thick. Sprinkle each side with salt and black pepper and set aside. Place the cassava flour, beaten eggs and breadcrumbs in separate shallow bowls. Take the steaks, dredge both sides in the cassava flour, dip them in the eggs and press each side into the breadcrumbs. Place them on a platter, cover and refrigerate for at least 30 minutes.

Meanwhile, make the gravy. You should have less than ⅓ cup (30 g) of cassava flour left on the plate. If there is more flour, then measure out ⅓ cup (30 g), or add more if there is less, and combine it with the chicken stock in a small saucepan. Whisk to mix. On medium heat, bring the gravy to a boil. When it's bubbling, lower the temperature and bring to a simmer while stirring with the whisk for 2 minutes, until the gravy thickens.

Preheat the air fryer to 360°F (180°C).

Place as many steaks as you can fit in the basket of the air fryer and set the timer for 12 minutes. Check for even cooking at 5 to 6 minutes and continue to cook until the timer goes off, or until the steak is no longer pink inside. Place the cooked steaks on a platter and keep them loosely covered until all the steaks are cooked.

When ready to serve, place the steaks on a plate, pour gravy over them, sprinkle with fresh black pepper and garnish with chopped fresh parsley. This is best served with Baked Potatoes (page 158) if you eat potatoes. If you do not eat white potatoes, Feisty Sweet Potatoes (page 121) make an awesome side, too.

Beef NEGIMAKI

The Japanese have a way of rolling food in seaweed and turning it into a work of art. So it's not surprising that scallion rolled in beef would be elegant and oh-so-tasty with teriyaki sauce. Have fun playing with your food with this one! Your kids might want to help out, too. Just warning ya.

COOK TIME: 6 MINUTES + 2–3 MINUTES STOVETOP COOKING ‖ SERVINGS: 4

24 scallions, cleaned and roots removed, plus more for tying

8 flattened flank steaks, at least 7–8" (18–20 cm) long on one side

1 cup (235 ml) Teriyaki Sauce (page 183)

½ cup (120 ml) organic sake

1 tsp sesame oil

1 tsp toasted sesame seeds, for garnish

In small saucepan, boil water with a pinch of salt. Blanch the scallions for 30 seconds and immediately plunge them into ice water. They should turn bright green and soft. Strain the water or blot the excess water, then lay the scallions on a plate and set aside.

Spread out the steaks on a cutting board and using a meat tenderizer or back of a chef's knife, flatten them out to be about ¼ inch (6 mm) thick, overlapping if necessary. Trim the steaks to about 6 x 4 inches (15 x 10 cm). Lay 3 scallions in the center of each and roll them up tightly, like sushi rolls. Tie the rolls toward one end with extra scallions, so they don't unravel. Use a toothpick to close the other end. Place the rolls and any meat scraps in a glass pan. Make the marinade by combining the teriyaki sauce, sake and sesame oil in a small bowl. Pour the marinade over the *negimaki* rolls and refrigerate for an hour.

Preheat the air fryer to 360°F (180°C).

When the air fryer reaches the desired temperature, place the negimaki rolls in the basket and set the timer for 6 minutes. Transfer any marinade left to a small saucepan and simmer for 2 minutes. Check on the rolls at 3 minutes. The rolls will cook very quickly. When the beef is brown and no longer pink, cut the rolls into 1-inch (2.5-cm) slices, like sushi. Place them on a serving platter, sprinkle with sesame seeds and serve with the warm teriyaki sauce from the pan. Serve with hot white rice or, if you don't eat rice, Cauli Couscous (page 172).

Note: You can also cut the rolls into slices first, put a skewer through them and cook according to the instructions above.

Stuffed CHIPOTLE POTATO SKINS

These are no ordinary game night, carb-heavy potato skins. These chipotle deviled eggs stuffed into crispy potato skins will tantalize anyone's taste buds! They are not only full of flavor but also nourishing, and you don't need beer to wash them down. That's not so bad, is it?

COOK TIME: 10 MINUTES || MAKES: 4 HALVES

2 medium-sized (about 7–9 oz [200–255 g] each) russet Baked Potatoes (page 158)

2 hard-boiled eggs, peeled and chopped (Eggs Three Ways, page 167)

2 tbsp (20 g) cooked bacon bits, divided (Baconomics, page 168)

¼ cup (60 ml) Homemade Mayo (page 180)

1 tsp Paleo chipotle hot sauce (or more if you want it spicier)

1 tsp or more chopped fresh parsley

Salt and black pepper to taste

¼ cup (60 ml) avocado oil, divided

1 tsp fresh chives and parsley, for garnish

Cut the baked potatoes in half lengthwise and scoop out some of the insides into a small mixing bowl while being careful not to rip the skin. Then, using a paring knife, cut the scooped-out potatoes into small pieces right in the bowl. Add the chopped hard-boiled eggs and half of the bacon bits to the potatoes.

Make the chipotle sauce by combining the Mayo, chipotle hot sauce, parsley, salt and pepper in a small bowl and mix well. If you don't have chipotle hot sauce, add chipotle pepper to any hot sauce. Okay, you don't want hot sauce? Then just add ground chipotle pepper to the mayo. There's no hard rule here as long as there's a chipotle flavor in the potato mixture.

Preheat the air fryer to 390°F (200°C).

Next, add the chipotle sauce to the bowl of potato and egg, coat them well and set aside. Take about 1 teaspoon of avocado oil, place it in your hand and rub a potato skin all over. This will make the skin crispy, so coat it well. Repeat this for the other three potato skin halves. Place the potato skins on a platter and fill them generously with the chipotle mixture. When the air fryer reaches 390°F (200°C), place the potato skins inside the basket, leaving some spaces in between them.

Set the timer for 8 minutes and cook until the timer goes off. Open the basket, sprinkle on the remaining bacon bits and continue to cook for 2 more minutes. When the timer goes off, take the stuffed potato skins out and place them on a platter. Sprinkle with chives and parsley, and serve immediately.

FINE, FEATHERED & FRIED

A while ago, I was a vegan for a year. Gasp! I know. But when I found out it wasn't the right diet for me and started to eat meat again, fried chicken was the first non-vegan meal I had. And oh boy, was that a meal I'll remember for the rest of my life! But on the Paleo diet, I couldn't eat fried chicken. Or so I thought. I knew it was going to be a challenge to make crispy Paleo-friendly fried chicken in the air fryer without dredging it in flour and deep-frying in a pot full of oil. But I took it on and yelped "Challenge accepted!" I mean, what's an air fryer cookbook if you can't find classic fried recipes, right? So, I fried countless drumsticks—which, by the way, should be the only fried chicken parts you eat, just saying.

I finally discovered the "secret" and it resulted in Not Your Gramma's Fried Chicken (page 76). It is juicy, tender on the inside and crispy on the outside, just as if they came out of the deep fryer, dripping with hot oil. But mine is with good fat and the taste is . . . well, I'll let you be the judge. But let me just say, proudly, that this recipe alone is worth the price of this book.

And don't forget the Easy Duck Confit (page 79). Who would have thought you can make duck confit in the air fryer? Just make sure to reserve the rendered duck fat for other yummy dishes you make.

Chicken is for kids of all ages, and who can forget the little ones who seem to put away a flock of chicken by eating only chicken tenders at every meal? My Chicken Tenders (page 84) can be served with ketchup for younger children, and with roasted garlic aioli for children ten and older. We don't age-discriminate.

Not YOUR GRAMMA'S FRIED CHICKEN

Who *hasn't* been taunted by the KFC commercials? I love fried chicken and hate those commercials. So, when writing this cookbook, I had to create this recipe for us all, the drooling KFC commercial haters. The "secret" coating in this recipe will give you crunchy and flavorful fried chicken that's even better than the KFC you've been missing in your life. The two-step method might sound like a lot for fried chicken but it's so worth the effort. There's a reason why this recipe made the cover. Trust me.

COOK TIME: 20 MINUTES || **SERVINGS: 6**

12 chicken drumsticks

½ tsp garlic powder

½ tsp onion powder

½ tsp sea salt

½ tsp paprika

1 tsp dried parsley

1 cup (150 g) Crispy Chicharrones crumbs (page 114)

Pat the drumsticks dry with paper towels and place them in a large zip-top bag. In a small bowl, combine all the seasonings and mix well. Put the seasoning in the zip-top bag and shake it up to coat all the drumsticks. Let it marinate in the refrigerator for 24 hours.

In a food processor, grind about 1 pound (450 g) of cooked Crispy Chicharrones to make 1 cup (150 g) of crumbs. Store in an airtight container until needed.

Preheat the air fryer to 360°F (180°C).

When you're ready to cook, transfer the crumbs to a plate. Take the drumsticks from the bag and press the crumbs into the meat. Refrigerate in a glass dish for 30 minutes. This process will make the crumbs stick to the meat when frying.

Place as many drumsticks as you can fit in the basket. Set the timer for 20 minutes. Check at 10 minutes and if needed, turn any drumsticks to cook evenly. When the timer goes off, insert a meat thermometer in the fattest part of the meat. The internal temperature should read at least 165°F (75°C). Repeat until all the drumsticks are done. Serve with Fancy Pants French Fries (page 118) or Feisty Sweet Potatoes (page 121).

Easy DUCK CONFIT

Unlike other fried food in this book, duck is cooked at a low temperature for a long time. The whole purpose of duck confit is to render the delicious duck fat while producing tender, fall-off-the-bone duck meat. So while my suggestion of 60 minutes might work for certain sizes of duck legs, you may have to adjust the time. Just make sure you use a meat thermometer to check that the internal temperature is 165°F (75°C). And reserve the duck fat in the drip basket for cooking other delicious dishes later.

COOK TIME: 60 MINUTES || SERVINGS: 4

1 tbsp (15 g) sea salt, divided

3 sprigs fresh thyme, roughly broken up

1 tsp fresh ground black pepper

3 tsp (6 g) dried thyme

1 shallot, chopped

3 cloves garlic, chopped

8 duck legs with thighs

1 tsp chopped fresh parsley, for garnish

Sprinkle ½ tablespoon (7.5 g) of the sea salt and the fresh thyme on a glass pan. Combine the remaining salt and the rest of the ingredients except the duck and parsley in a small bowl and mix well. Place the duck legs in the glass pan, pull the duck skin away from the meat and create a pocket. Tuck the seasonings in the pocket evenly between the skin and the meat. Sprinkle any leftover seasonings on top. Cover and refrigerate for 24 hours.

Preheat the air fryer to 270°F (130°C).

When the air fryer reaches the desired temperature, place all the legs in the basket, skin side up. Overlapping the legs is fine since you will have to rearrange them halfway through. Set the timer for 30 minutes. When the timer goes off, using oven mitts, carefully take out the drip basket and the wire basket and place them on a heat resistant surface. Take the wired basket out, strain the duck fat from the bottom basket into a bowl with a lid, and reserve for your other cooking needs. Swap the legs on top with the ones on the bottom. Place the basket in the drip basket and put them back in the air fryer. Check to make sure the temperature is 270°F (130°C) and set the timer for 30 minutes. Cook until the timer goes off. The skin should be crispy and the internal temperature near the bone should be 165°F (75°C). Strain the duck fat into the bowl again. Sprinkle with fresh parsley and serve immediately.

Chicken TANDOORI WITH LIME AND CILANTRO CAULI COUSCOUS

Traditional Indian chicken tandoori is marinated in Indian spices and then cooked in a very hot, clay tandoor oven. This recipe has all the right spices in the marinade to tantalize your taste buds with deep flavors. And cooking them in the air fryer with the proximity of the heat source makes the chicken taste like it was cooked in the tandoor oven just the same. Serve with lime and cilantro cauli couscous and you're set for a night of Indian fare!

COOK TIME: 20 MINUTES || SERVINGS: 4

COCONUT MILK YOGURT MARINADE

1 cup (235 g) full-fat coconut milk yogurt

3 tbsp (25 g) onion powder

2 tsp (10 g) grated fresh ginger

5 cloves garlic, minced

3 tsp (45 g) garam masala

1 tsp turmeric

2 tsp (5 g) cumin

2 tsp (5 g) coriander powder

2 tsp (5 g) cayenne pepper

2 tsp (5 g) smoked or regular paprika

1 tsp sea salt

8 chicken drumsticks

LIME AND CILANTRO CAULI COUSCOUS

Cauli Couscous (page 172)

2 tbsp (30 ml) lime juice

1 tbsp (2.5 g) chopped fresh cilantro

¼ tsp curry powder

Combine the marinade ingredients in a small bowl and mix well. Put the drumsticks in a glass container with a lid and pour in the marinade. Move the drumsticks around in the marinade and coat them well. Refrigerate for 1 to 2 days.

Preheat the air fryer to 360°F (180°C).

Mix the Cauli Couscous, lime juice, cilantro and curry powder in a bowl, cover and refrigerate until serving.

Take the drumsticks out of the refrigerator and shake off any excess sauce. Place the drumsticks in the basket and set the timer for 20 minutes. At 10 minutes, turn any drumsticks over to cook more evenly, if needed. Brush more marinade over the drumsticks and cook until the timer goes off. Take the drumsticks out, then insert a meat thermometer to make sure that the internal temperature is at least 165°F (75°C). Let the drumsticks rest for 5 minutes before serving with lime and cilantro cauli couscous.

Lemon THYME CHICKEN BREASTS

Lemon and thyme are a match made in heaven. These delicately herbed chicken breasts can be served as a meal or be used in other dishes, like Savory Sweet Potato Stacks (page 36). Regardless how you devour this classic chicken dish, it will be juicy and tender when cooked in the air fryer. Make sure to buy bone-in breasts for extra flavor.

COOK TIME: 30 MINUTES || SERVINGS: 2

2 tbsp (30 ml) avocado oil

1 tbsp (1.5 g) dried thyme

2 tsp (10 g) salt

Juice from 1 lemon

2 (1–1½ lb) bone-in chicken breasts

In a large glass container with a lid, combine all the ingredients except the chicken and mix well. Add the chicken breasts and coat all sides. Marinate for 24 hours.

Preheat the air fryer to 360°F (180°C).

Place the chicken breasts, skin side up, in the basket and set the timer for 30 minutes. Check at 15 minutes to make sure the chicken is browning evenly. Cook until the internal temperature is at least 165°F (75°C) when the meat thermometer is inserted in the thickest part of the meat. Let it rest for 5 minutes before serving.

Chicken TENDERS WITH ROASTED GARLIC AIOLI

Chicken tenders are everyone's favorite, and this Paleo version of crispy, breaded tenders are perfect to serve with roasted garlic aioli or ketchup. Make batches and freeze them ahead of time to reheat in the air fryer for a quick meal. Or just bread the chicken and freeze them to cook when needed.

COOK TIME: 25 MINUTES || SERVINGS: 2

8 chicken tenderloin strips, or strips cut from chicken breasts

¼ cup (25 g) cassava flour (I use Otto's Cassava Flour)

¼ tsp sea salt

1 tsp cayenne pepper

½ tsp black pepper

2 large eggs, beaten

1 cup (150 g) Italian Breadcrumbs (page 187)

ROASTED GARLIC AIOLI

2 cloves Roasted Garlic (page 171)

½ cup (120 ml) Homemade Mayo (page 180)

1 tbsp (15 ml) extra-virgin olive oil (EVOO)

½ tbsp (7 ml) lemon juice

⅛ tsp sea salt

1 tsp cayenne pepper

Place the chicken on a cutting board and, using a meat tenderizer or the back of a chef's knife, flatten the tenderloins until they are ¼ inch (6 mm) thick and then set aside. Mix the cassava flour, sea salt, cayenne pepper and black pepper. Place the cassava flour mixture on a plate, the beaten eggs in a shallow bowl and the breadcrumbs on another plate. Dredge the chicken in the flour, dip them in the eggs and press the breadcrumbs into the meat. Place the dredged chicken tenders on a plate, cover and refrigerate for 30 minutes.

Preheat the air fryer to 360°F (180°C).

Place all the chicken tenders in the air fryer basket and set the timer for 25 minutes. Meanwhile, make the roasted garlic aioli by combining all the ingredients in a food processor and pulsing a few times until all the ingredients are well blended. Transfer the aioli to a small serving bowl and set aside. When the timer goes off and the inside of the chicken is opaque white, serve immediately with roasted garlic aioli.

SWIMMERS & SLIMERS

If I had a choice between seafood and desserts, I'd pick seafood. I know, I'm weird. I mean, don't get me wrong. I would devour any kind of crème brûlée, like the Pumpkin Coconut Crème Brûlée on page 150, but for nourishment, I'd choose lobsters and shrimp over sweets. I mean, how can you refuse Lobster Mac and Cheese (page 99) or the classic Coconut Shrimp with a tropical dipping sauce (page 107)? And while we're on shellfish, I'm hooked on scallops. I always cooked scallops in a hot, buttered cast-iron skillet and never thought air frying them was even "legal." I mean, what chef with a sound mind would even think of air frying them? Blasphemy! Well, call me a rebel rouser, but I legalized it with the Bacon-Wrapped Sea Scallops (page 88). Trust me on this. Not a shellfish fan? Quick and Easy Calamari on Fire (page 96) was tricky, but this dish is hot! Figuratively and literally. And Cajun Fish Fry (page 100) has a bit of Southern flare that will make you think you're lazily lounging on a fishing boat in the bayou.

Whatever seafood you're in the mood for, there are enough choices in this section to satisfy anyone!

Bacon-WRAPPED SEA SCALLOPS

My daughter doesn't like scallops, yet she'll devour bacon-wrapped sea scallops. But when I make them on the cast-iron skillet, the grease splatters everywhere. Not in the air fryer! Make these, and they'll be the hit of the party while making you look like you slaved over the stove all day.

COOK TIME: 15 MINUTES || SERVINGS: 4

Cauli Coucous (page 172)

1 tbsp (2 g) chopped fresh basil

½ of a lemon

8 uncured bacon strips

8 large sea scallops

3 tsp (10 g) chopped pine nuts

1 tsp balsamic glaze

1 lemon wedge, for topping

Mix the Cauli Couscous and the chopped basil and squeeze half a lemon on top. Mix and refrigerate until serving.

Bring the bacon to room temperature, then cut the strips in half lengthwise, trimming the fatty bottom half, and place the less fatty halves on a plate. I know . . . bacon fat is good for you, but there is plenty of fat on this bacon for this recipe. Besides, you don't want too much fat in the air fryer or else it burns the bacon. Or the machine. Wrap the bacon around each scallop with a small overlap and use a toothpick to secure it. Try to pierce the scallop from one side all the way through to the other side, so the bacon stays in place.

Preheat the air fryer to 390°F (200°C).

When the air fryer reaches 390°F (200°C), place 4 scallops in the basket, leaving some space between each scallop. Set the timer for 12 minutes. Halfway through, open the basket and turn the scallops over. When the timer goes off, sprinkle some chopped pine nuts on top of each scallop and cook for 3 more minutes or until the nuts are brown. When the scallops are done, set the batch on a platter and keep them covered. Place the next batch of 4 scallops in the basket and repeat. When the last batch is done, put the scallops on the platter with the first batch and drizzle with balsamic glaze and lemon juice from 1 lemon wedge before serving with the Cauli Couscous.

$\mathcal{Salmon}$ WITH GINGER SAUCE

My husband grew up in the Pacific Northwest—salmon country. Before I met him, I rarely had salmon. But, since his favorite salmon dish is his mom's steamed salmon with ginger and scallions, I learned to perfect it over the years. With my children's allergies to soy, I had to Paleotize it with coconut aminos. And now, he prefers it my way! Instead of steaming the salmon, baking it in the air fryer caramelizes the ginger sauce and makes the salmon a bit sweet and deliciously aromatic. I usually serve it with white rice, but you can serve it with Baked Potatoes (page 158) or Cauli Couscous (page 172), or on a bed of spring greens. It just may become your family's favorite, too.

COOK TIME: 15 MINUTES || SERVINGS: 2

2 large wild-caught salmon fillets, about ½ lb (230 g) each

2 tsp (10 g) sea salt

¼ cup (60 ml) coconut aminos

2 tbsp (30 g) grated fresh ginger

1 scallion, chopped, for garnish

Take the salmon fillets out and pat them dry. Place them in an ovenproof deep dish or skillet and sprinkle each with 1 teaspoon of sea salt. Mix the coconut aminos and ginger in a small bowl and pour over the salmon fillets.

Preheat the air fryer to 360°F (180°C).

Place the skillet or deep dish in the basket and set the timer for 15 minutes, or until the salmon is firm. Spoon the ginger sauce from the bottom of the skillet or dish over the salmon fillets and garnish with scallions before serving.

Teriyaki SQUID

Squid is one of my favorite seafoods to cook because it's quick to make and is allergy-proof! My son loves this dish since he's allergic to shellfish but can have squid without any issues. And he loves the teriyaki sauce! Marinate the squid in the sake marinade as long as you can for a richer flavor. If you don't have time to marinate, drizzle on extra teriyaki sauce before serving.

COOK TIME: 7 MINUTES ‖ SERVINGS: 2

2 large whole squid, with or without tentacles, cleaned

2 tsp (10 g) grated fresh ginger

2 tbsp (30 ml) sake

2 tbsp (30 ml) coconut aminos

1 tbsp (15 ml) fish sauce

2 tbsp (30 ml) Teriyaki Sauce (page 183)

1 tbsp (15 ml) avocado oil, for brushing the air fryer basket

Combine the squid, ginger, sake, coconut aminos and fish sauce in a glass pan that can fit the squid. Cover and marinate for at least 1 to 4 hours.

Brush the basket with avocado oil and preheat the air fryer to 390°F (200°C).

Take the squid from the refrigerator, strain the marinade into a small saucepan and pat the squid dry. Place them in the basket and set the timer for 7 minutes. Add the Teriyaki Sauce to the saucepan with the marinade and stir. Bring to a boil and then lower the temperature to keep warm, right before serving. When the timer goes off, take the squid out of the basket and place them on a serving dish. Drizzle with the teriyaki-marinade mixture and serve immediately over hot white rice or, if you don't eat rice, Cauli Couscous (page 172).

CRAB

Lump crab meat with horseradish in this quintessential New England dish makes this recipe one of my family's favorites. Serve with horseradish aioli and a side of greens, and you'll feel like you've been teleported to Martha's Vineyard, Massachusetts.

COOK TIME: 10 MINUTES || SERVINGS: 4

2 tbsp (30 ml) Homemade Mayo (page 180)

1 tbsp (15 g) grated fresh horseradish

2 tbsp (10 g) coconut flour

2 large eggs, beaten

½ cup (75 g) finely chopped celery

¼ cup (60 g) finely chopped shallot

½ cup (75 g) finely chopped red bell pepper

1 tbsp (3 g) chopped fresh chives

1 tsp dried tarragon

1 tsp dry mustard powder

¼ tsp sea salt

¼ tsp black pepper

1 lb (450 g) lump crab meat

1 tbsp (15 ml) extra-virgin olive oil (EVOO), for brushing the basket

2 tbsp (5 g) chopped fresh parsley, divided

HORSERADISH AIOLI

⅓ cup (80 ml) Homemade Mayo (page 180)

1 tsp grated fresh horseradish, or more for more heat

1 tsp pickle relish

2 cloves garlic, minced

Sea salt and black pepper to taste

Combine all the ingredients, except the crab meat, EVOO and 1 tablespoon (2.5 g) of parsley, in a large mixing bowl. Add the crab meat next and incorporate it in but don't overmix. You want the meat to stay intact as much as possible while blending in the spices and herbs. Make 4 patties similar in thickness, place them on a plate, cover and refrigerate for 30 minutes.

Preheat the air fryer to 360°F (180°C).

When the air fryer reaches the desired temperature, brush the basket with EVOO and place the crab cakes in the basket. Set the timer for 10 minutes.

Meanwhile, make the horseradish aioli by combining all the ingredients in a small bowl. When the timer goes off, take the crab cakes out, garnish with the remaining chopped parsley and serve immediately with horseradish aioli.

Quick AND EASY CALAMARI ON FIRE

My family loves fried calamari and spicy peppers so I Paleotized this classic. You can leave out the peppers if you don't want the heat but why would you? Live a little.

COOK TIME: 10–12 MINUTES ‖ SERVINGS: 2

3 squid bodies and tentacles

1 medium onion, sliced

1 jalapeño pepper, thinly sliced

1 tbsp (15 ml) extra-virgin olive oil

BATTER

½ cup (50 g) cassava flour

¼ cup (25 g) potato flour

½ tsp baking soda

1 tsp cream of tartar

½ tsp onion powder

2 cups (475 ml) cold water

DREDGE FLOUR

½ cup (50 g) cassava flour

½ tsp garlic powder

½ tsp baking soda

½ tsp cream of tartar

WARM CALAMARI SAUCE

1 cup (245 g) tomato puree

1 tbsp (10 g) chopped onion

1 clove garlic, minced

1 tsp chopped fresh parsley

1 tsp red pepper flakes

⅛ tsp sea salt

⅛ tsp black pepper

Slice the squid bodies to ½ inch (13 mm) thickness and cut large tentacles in half lengthwise. You should have about 2 cups (300 g) of sliced squid. Set aside. Mix the ingredients for the batter together and put in a shallow bowl. Mix the ingredients for the dredge flour and put on a plate. Set the batter and dredge flour dishes side by side. It's really important to keep the flour dry so don't use the same hand or tongs for the batter and dredging.

First, coat the squid, onion and pepper slices in the dredging flour and then dip in the batter. Then coat them in the dredge flour again. Place them on a large plate in a single layer—as many as possible. Cover and refrigerate for 30 minutes. Spray the air fryer basket with the EVOO and preheat the air fryer to 390°F (200°C).

Take the squid, onion and pepper slices out of the refrigerator and shake off any excess batter and flour. Place them in the basket and set the timer for 10 minutes. Some of the batter or flour will fall through to the bottom. That's okay. You should have plenty of batter still on the squid. You will also have to put them on top of each other, and that's okay, too. Just rearrange them at 5 minutes, so they are cooked thoroughly. If they are not cooked at 10 minutes, cook for 2 more minutes. These will not be "deep-fried" crispy, but they should still be crispy, especially around the edges.

Meanwhile, make the calamari sauce in a small saucepan by mixing all the ingredients and bringing it to a boil. When the sauce bubbles, lower the heat and keep it warm.

When the air fryer timer goes off, take out the squid, onions and peppers and plate them all mixed up. Serve immediately with a side of warm calamari sauce.

Lobster MAC AND CHEESE

Being New Yorkers who never saw lobsters smaller than 2 pounds (900 g), my family and I were disappointed that the lobsters in a local Maine lobster shack were "puny" little 1 to 1½ pounders (450 to 680 g). They told us that the smaller ones taste better, and they were right—I had the best tasting lobster in my life! That's why we use 1 to 1½ pound (450 to 680 g) lobsters in this recipe.

This "cheese" sauce for Paleo eaters can be challenging to make but it will satisfy even the non-Paleo eaters. Prepare the lobster meat and the sauce ahead of time and assemble them for an unforgettable meal that will become everyone's favorite!

COOK TIME: 15 MINUTES || SERVINGS: 2

---

3 (1–1½ lbs [450–680 g]) live lobsters (should yield 1½–2 lbs [680–900 g] of lobster meat)

5 cups (1.15 L) water

1 large head of cauliflower

2 cups (460 g) Paleo "Cheese" Sauce (page 184)

2 tbsp (10 g) extra fine blanched almond flour, for topping

1 tbsp (3 g) chopped fresh parsley, for garnish

Once you bring the lobsters home from the fish monger, put them in the freezer for about 15 to 20 minutes. Meanwhile, put the water in a stockpot with a steamer and bring it to a boil. Take the lobsters from the freezer, clean the shells with a brush and put them on a cutting board on their bellies. With a sharp knife, pierce between the head and the body. Flip them over and cut down in the middle of the belly from the upper body toward the tail. You may see some reflexive movements but at this point, the lobster is not in pain. This is the most humane way to kill the lobsters because they die instantly, and the legs should go limp. Put the lobsters in the pot and steam for 10 minutes, or until the shells turn bright red.

Meanwhile, clean the cauliflower, discard the outer leaves and cut the cauliflower in half. When the lobsters are done, take them out and set into a large mixing bowl. Put the cauliflower halves in the pot and steam for 5 to 8 minutes or until soft but not mushy. Meanwhile, cut the lobster tails from the bodies. Make a slit at the end of the lobster tail and, using your finger, push the meat out. Cut the lobster tail meat into chunks, about the size of macaroni pasta. Repeat the process with the rest of the lobster tails and put the meat in a large mixing bowl. Reserve the rest of the lobsters for later use. When the cauliflower is done, cut the florets into macaroni-size pieces. Add them to the bowl with the lobster meat. Add the cheese sauce and mix well. Transfer the mixture to an ovenproof deep dish, sprinkle almond flour on top and loosely cover with aluminum foil.

Preheat the air fryer to 360°F (180°C). Place the dish in the basket, and set the timer for 10 minutes. When the timer goes off, open the basket, remove the foil and set the timer for an additional 5 minutes. Cook until the top is browned or until the timer goes off. Garnish with chopped parsley and serve immediately.

Cajun FISH FRY

Cajun spices add color to a boring pallet of plain ole fish. You can use classic Southern fish like catfish, but cod or haddock works great, too. Serve with horseradish aioli (page 95) for an extra kick!

COOK TIME: 10 MINUTES || SERVINGS: 4

---

1 lb (450 g) fillet of your favorite fish, like catfish, cod or haddock (whole perch is okay, too)

1½ tsp (8 g) sea salt, divided

1 tsp paprika

1 tsp cayenne pepper

1 tsp garlic powder

½ tsp onion powder

½ cup (30 g) Italian Breadcrumbs (page 187)

2 large eggs, beaten

½ cup (50 g) cassava flour (I use Otto's Cassava Flour)

CAJUN TARTAR SAUCE

½ cup (120 ml) Homemade Mayo (page 180)

1 tbsp (15 ml) Paleo ketchup

¼ tsp cumin

¼ tsp cayenne pepper

⅛ tsp black pepper

1 tbsp (15 ml) pickle relish

1 tbsp (15 ml) extra-virgin olive oil (EVOO), for brushing the basket

Normally, you should fry a whole fish, like catfish, perch or haddock. But if you are using a large, meaty fish like cod, you can slice it about 1 inch (2.5 cm) thick. Pat the fish fillets dry and sprinkle with ½ teaspoon of sea salt on both sides and set aside.

Mix the paprika, cayenne pepper, garlic powder, onion powder, breadcrumbs and 1 teaspoon of sea salt in a small bowl. Place the beaten egg in a shallow bowl, and the breadcrumbs mixture and cassava flour on two separate plates. Coat the fillets in the cassava flour, dip in the eggs and coat well with the breadcrumbs. Place the coated fillets in the refrigerator for at least 30 minutes.

Preheat the air fryer to 360°F (180°C).

Make the Cajun tartar sauce by mixing all the ingredients and set it aside.

Take the fish from the refrigerator. Brush the basket with EVOO. Carefully, place as many fish fillets as you can in the basket. Set the timer for 10 minutes. When the timer goes off, take the fish fillets out with a spatula. Repeat until the fish fillets are cooked. Serve immediately with the Cajun tartar sauce.

 *Fish* TOSTADAS

Taco Tuesdays will never be the same when you serve your family these Fish Tostadas. These crispy tostadas are like opened tacos and they are even more fun to eat when you can pile on all kinds of fresh veggies. Put out a spread like a buffet and let each family member choose! It's a great way to add more veggies to their diet.

COOK TIME: 10 MINUTES || SERVINGS: 2

2 Tostadas (page 176)

1 tsp cumin

½ tsp paprika

¼ tsp cayenne pepper

¼ tsp garlic powder

⅛ tsp salt

1 lb (450 g) haddock or cod, cut into 1" (2.5-cm) chunks

1 tbsp (15 ml) extra-virgin olive oil (EVOO), for brushing inside the basket

CILANTRO CREAM

¼ cup (60 ml) Homemade Mayo (page 180)

¼ cup (10 g) chopped fresh cilantro

1 tsp lime juice

1 tsp lime zest

1 clove garlic, minced

1 tsp finely chopped jalapeño pepper

FILLINGS

Chopped tomatoes, shredded cabbage, cucumbers, green bell peppers, purple onion and cilantro

Make the tostadas 5 to 6 inches (13 to 15 cm) in diameter and set aside. Combine the cumin, paprika, cayenne, garlic and salt in a medium-sized mixing bowl. Add the fish chunks to the bowl and mix. Marinate for about an hour at room temperature.

Preheat the air fryer to 360°F (180°C).

Meanwhile, mix all the ingredients for the cilantro cream in a small bowl and refrigerate until serving.

Brush the basket with the EVOO. Place the fish chunks in the basket and set the timer for 10 minutes. Check at 5 minutes and move the fish around, if needed, to make sure all the pieces cook evenly. When the timer goes off, place the fish on a platter and keep them covered. Put the tostadas in the air fryer to keep them warm and crispy until all the fillings are prepared. Put each filling in a separate bowl, take the cilantro cream from the refrigerator and take the tostadas out of the air fryer. Let your family assemble the tacos with fillings they like!

Note: You can make the tostadas ahead of time and store them in an airtight container. When ready to eat, reheat them in the air fryer for 3 minutes right before serving.

Easy CRAB AND SUN-DRIED TOMATO QUICHE

Quiche is one of the easiest breakfasts or lunches to make, and with the air fryer it's even easier, if that's possible. These personal-sized quiches have delicate crab flavors and contrasting sun-dried tomatoes, which go well together. Make some ahead of time and freeze for busy mornings. The cook time may look scary, but it's hands-off. And if you're short on time, cut the ingredients (and time) in half for one serving.

COOK TIME: 66–70 MINUTES ‖ SERVINGS: 2

CRUST

2 cups (190 g) extra fine blanched almond flour

1 large egg, beaten

2 tbsp (30 g) ghee, softened at room temperature

FILLING

1 cup (450 g) lump crab meat

2 tbsp (20 g) chopped sun-dried tomatoes

2 tsp (4 g) chopped fresh tarragon

8 large eggs, beaten

1 cup (240 ml) unsweetened almond milk

½ tsp sea salt

½ tsp black pepper

2 tbsp (5 g) chopped fresh parsley, plus more for garnish

For the crust, combine all the ingredients in a small mixing bowl. Press down the crust mixture into two separate ovenproof dishes or skillets. Using a fork, poke a few holes into the bottom of the crust. Place one of the dishes or skillets in the basket and heat the air fryer to 360°F (180°C). Bake for about 3 to 5 minutes. Take out the dish when the crust is brown and set aside to cool. Put in the second dish or skillet and bake until the crust is brown.

In a medium-sized mixing bowl, combine all the ingredients for the filling. Transfer half of the mixture to one dish with the baked crust and pour the rest into the second dish. Cover one dish and refrigerate it to cook later. Put the other dish back into the basket, turn the air fryer on to 360°F (180°C) and set the timer to 30 minutes. Bake until the timer goes off or when a toothpick comes out clean when inserted in the middle. Cook the second dish for 30 minutes. Serve hot with chopped parsley as a garnish.

Coconut SHRIMP

Just about everyone I know loves coconut shrimp. But of course, they are usually deep-fried, and if you have stomach issues, you may not be able to enjoy them. Once you make them in the air fryer, you will be glad you bought the machine. This recipe alone is worth the appliance. Make the dipping sauce ahead of time and serve it on the side. Also, make sure to buy only wild-caught shrimp and not farmed shrimp, especially from Asia. Your body will thank you.

COOK TIME: 14 MINUTES ‖ MAKES: 12 SHRIMP

12 wild-caught XL shrimp

⅓ cup (30 g) cassava flour (I like Otto's Cassava Flour)

2 large eggs, beaten

½ cup (40 g) unsweetened shredded coconut

1 tbsp (15 ml) extra-virgin olive oil (EVOO), for brushing the basket

1 lime wedge

TROPICAL DIPPING SAUCE

1 cup (235 ml) pineapple juice

4 tsp (20 ml) coconut aminos

1 tsp raw honey

¼ tsp ginger powder

½ tsp tapioca flour

Wash the shrimp and devein them. Make small slits in the belly of the shrimp, so they don't curl when cooked. Put the cassava flour on a plate, the eggs in a shallow bowl and the shredded coconut on another plate. Dredge the shrimp in the flour, dip in the egg and roll and coat with the shredded coconut. Refrigerate in a glass dish for 30 minutes.

Preheat the air fryer to 360°F (180°C).

Brush the basket with EVOO. Place 6 shrimp in the basket in a single layer and set the timer for 7 minutes.

Meanwhile, in a small saucepan, bring the pineapple juice to a boil and then simmer on low heat until it's reduced to half. Add the rest of the ingredients and stir well. Take the pan off the heat and set aside.

When the timer goes off, take the shrimp out, place them on a plate and cover. Put the rest of the shrimp in the basket and cook for 7 minutes. When the timer goes off, squeeze some lime juice on the shrimp and serve immediately with the tropical dipping sauce.

Note: This recipe works really well with chicken tenders, too. Flatten out chicken tenderloins or cut chicken breasts in 3-inch (7.6-cm)-wide strips for this recipe.

MIDNIGHT MUNCHIES

Studies have shown that those who pull late nighters and watch TV for hours and hours tend to gain weight. We all get the munchies if we stay up late and we tend to reach for a snack when mindlessly watching TV.

I think the main problem is not that you're snacking, but that you're snacking on the wrong foods. So, I created these snack recipes to help you ward off weight issues for snacking at night. But don't blame me if you want to stay up just to eat these Midnight Munchies. Remember to snack responsibly.

But seriously, if you don't make anything else in this book, you have to make the Korean Beef Jerky (page 113) and Crispy Chicharrones (page 114). Not in the mood for meat? Try the Sour Cream and Onion Kale Chips (page 110). You couldn't make them fast enough! Promise.

Sour CREAM AND ONION KALE CHIPS

Don't let anyone tell you kale is no longer trendy. Not until you try this dairy-free Paleo version of everyone's favorite "sour cream and onion"–flavored chips. These are tangy and onion-y and so quick to make in the air fryer. These chips make a perfect midnight or midday snack and you will never go back to buying kale chips from the store again. Just make sure you place a stainless steel rack on top of the kale leaves so they don't get swept around while frying.

COOK TIME: 4–6 MINUTES || SERVINGS: 2

1 bunch curly kale

½ cup (75 g) raw cashews, soaked for 24 hours

½ small onion

1 tbsp (15 ml) apple cider vinegar

1 tsp sea salt

Take the kale leaves off the stems and wash thoroughly. Take the leaves out of the water, drain the water and repeat until there is no debris in the water. Use a salad spinner to dry the kale leaves as much as possible. Spread the leaves out on a clean kitchen towel and pat dry. Place the kale in a large bowl and set aside.

In a food processor, combine the cashews, onion, apple cider vinegar and sea salt and puree until smooth.

Preheat the air fryer to 300°F (150°C).

Pour the cashew puree into the bowl of kale leaves and gently massage it into the leaves with your hands, coating them as well as you can. Place the kale leaves in the basket and spread them out. To prevent the leaves from flying around in the basket, place a small wire rack on top of the leaves. Set the timer for 4 minutes. Check for doneness when the timer goes off. If not yet crispy, set the timer for another 2 minutes. The kale chips can be stored in an airtight container for up to one week—if they last that long!

Korean BEEF JERKY

This classic protein snack is my son's favorite. I can't keep these in the house for more than a day. They are baked slowly on low heat to ensure even cooking but they still cook faster in the air fryer than in the oven. They make a great midday snack for a quick mojo "picker-upper" without making you crash the way carb-loaded snacks do.

COOK TIME: 60–70 MINUTES + 2 MINUTES STOVETOP COOKING || MAKES: 1 POUND (450 G)

1 lb (450 g) sirloin tips or boneless short rib meat or any meat with marbleized fat

1 tbsp (10 g) arrowroot or tapioca flour

1 tbsp (15 ml) water

MARINADE

½ cup (120 ml) coconut aminos

¼ cup (60 ml) raw honey

2 tbsp (30 ml) blackstrap molasses

½ tsp ground ginger

½ tsp garlic powder

½ tsp black pepper

1 tbsp (10 g) red pepper flakes

½ cup (120 ml) water

2 tsp (7 g) toasted sesame seeds

Put the meat in the freezer for at least 20 minutes for easier slicing. Meanwhile, make a slurry with the arrowroot or tapioca flour and water and set aside. In a small pan, combine the marinade ingredients, except for the sesame seeds, on low heat. Add the slurry and stir for 2 minutes or until it thickens. Add the sesame seeds, turn the heat off and cool.

Take the meat out of the freezer and cut it into ½-inch (13-mm)-wide strips, preferably 5 inches (13 cm) long. Using a meat tenderizer, flatten out the meat, but not too much. Put the meat and the cooled marinade in an airtight glass container and mix well. Close the lid and marinate overnight in the refrigerator.

Preheat the air fryer to 220°F (105°C) and place it in a well-ventilated area. Place the meat in the basket in a single layer. It's okay if they overlap a little as the meat will shrink as it cooks. Put a rack over the first layer and put more meat strips on the rack. Set the timer for 60 minutes. Put the rest of the meat back in the refrigerator until the second batch has to be cooked. You can either cook all the meat or divide it in half and cook the second batch later. Uncooked beef in the marinade should be good for a few days in the refrigerator but no more than 3 days.

Check the meat at 30 minutes and move the pieces around for even cooking. Continue cooking until the timer goes off. The meat should be between dehydrated and cooked but not totally dry. You should feel the wet sauce on the outside, and the meat should be a little stiff but not brittle. And if not all the meat is done, take out the ones that are cooked and leave the softer ones in to cook for another 10 minutes. If you want more spiciness, sprinkle on more red pepper flakes as soon as you take them out of the air fryer. Store the beef jerky at room temperature up to 1 day but after 24 hours, store them in the refrigerator if you have any left.

Crispy CHICHARRONES

The first time I had *chicharrones*, I thought it was strange. The thought of chewing on deep-fried pork fat didn't sound very appealing, but I became addicted. I loved the crispy and meaty crunch with every bite and the subtle, briny taste got me wanting more as I licked the plate clean. I created this recipe from that memory, so you can enjoy it like I did, not only as a snack, but also to use as the secret ingredient to make fried dishes crispy, like Not Your Gramma's Fried Chicken (page 76) and Crispy Garlicky Pork Chops (page 67). You can use pork belly with skin or without skin. Just make sure they are cooked crispy all around when you fry them.

COOK TIME: 30–40 MINUTES || MAKES: 3–4 CUPS (450–600 G)

1 tsp cumin

1 tsp garlic powder

1 tsp onion powder

½ tsp sea salt

1 tsp dried oregano

2 lbs (900 g) pork belly, with or without skin

Note: This recipe might make the air fryer get smoky because of the dripping fat so be sure to put the air fryer in a well-ventilated area. You can drain the fat from the dripping basket if the air fryer gets smoky.

In a small bowl, combine all the ingredients except the pork belly and mix. Transfer the seasonings to a large zip-top bag.

Cut the pork belly in ½ x 2–inch (13 mm x 5–cm) pieces and put them in the zip-top bag with the seasonings. Shake the bag and mix the seasonings into the pork belly pieces to make sure all the pieces are coated well. Marinate overnight in the refrigerator.

Preheat the air fryer to 360°F (180°C) and place it in a well-ventilated area.

Take the pork belly from the refrigerator and place half of it in the basket. The meat pieces will overlap but spread them out as best as you can. Close the basket and cook for 10 minutes. Open the basket and mix the pieces with tongs. Close the basket and cook for another 10 minutes. Open the basket again and mix the pieces, making sure the pieces are not burnt. You should see the pieces browning and shrinking to smaller sizes. Close the basket and cook for another 10 minutes or until all the pieces are crispy. Take this batch out, place in a bowl and cook the remaining pork belly the same way.

Chicharrones are great for snacking when served immediately or store in an airtight glass container up to 2 weeks in the refrigerator or in the freezer for up to 1 month.

PASSIONATELY PALETARIAN

"Paletarian" is pretty straight-forward: Paleo + vegetarian. In this section, I highlight the plants we love to eat but can't because many of them are deep-fried.

Take vegetable tempura for example. It's very challenging to create a Paleo batter that will stick to the vegetables. And to fry using air—not frying in deep hot oil—and still have the batter stay on the vegetables was twice as difficult. But I finally managed to create the perfect tempura batter on page 127.

How about French fries, the iconic American fast food? My Fancy Pants French Fries (page 118) will make you wish you bought the air fryer sooner. They are crispy on the outside, soft on the inside and the fancy pants topping will make you think they are from a Michelin-starred restaurant.

Can't have white potatoes? Don't worry. I got you covered with Yuca au Gratin (page 122). These taste just like white potatoes without the starch and they are not part of the nightshade family; not to mention, my "cheese" sauce will fool you into thinking you're cheating.

And if you've been staying away from deep-fried foods, you will love how the air fryer turns out classic vegetable dishes, like Healthy Onion Rings (page 139), Quick and Easy Fried Pickles (page 131), Fried Avocados (page 140) and even Feisty Sweet Potatoes (page 121) that never get crispy when baked in the oven.

So when you hear people criticizing how Paleo people ONLY eat meat, say you are a Paletarian and proudly produce these yummylicious recipes, whipped up in the air fryer and using fresh vegetables without junky oils and grains.

Fancy Pants FRENCH FRIES

French fries are one of the first foods that comes to mind when I think of fried food. And can you blame me? Who doesn't love hot, crispy and crunchy fries? Since we don't fry in oil, I tried baking them in the oven, but they rarely meet my standard of crispiness. But in the air fryer, it never fails with a little trick I'm going to share with you. We make these fries often and they always come out crispy. Make them extra special with my fancy pants oil, and they will go with practically everything!

COOK TIME: 12 MINUTES || SERVINGS: 4

---

4 large russet potatoes, cut into ¼" (6-mm)-thick fries

1 tbsp (15 ml) extra-virgin olive oil (EVOO)

1 clove garlic, minced

3 tbsp (45 ml) good quality truffle oil

1 tsp chopped fresh parsley

1 tsp sea salt

Wash the potatoes well to discard any dirt and debris from the skin. I like fries with skin on them but if you don't, you can peel them. Cut the potatoes into regular-sized fries. The secret to making crispy fries is to eliminate as much starch from the potatoes as you can, so soak the cut potatoes in cold water for at least 30 minutes; change the water when it gets cloudy, about twice. The longer you soak them in cold water, the more starch will dissipate, resulting in crispier fries.

Preheat the air fryer to 360°F (180°C).

Strain the fries and spread them on a clean kitchen towel. Pat them dry as well as you can and transfer to a large mixing bowl. Add the EVOO to the fries and coat them well with your hands. Place the fries in the basket and set the timer for 12 minutes. At 6 minutes, shake the basket to move the fries around.

In a small bowl, mix the garlic, truffle oil, parsley and sea salt and set aside. Finish frying the fries until the timer goes off. Check to see if the fries are done and cook some more if needed. Transfer the fries to a serving plate, garnish with the garlic truffle oil mixture and serve immediately.

Feisty SWEET POTATOES

Sweet potatoes contain a lot of moisture and they rarely come out crispy if baked in the oven. The only way to ensure sweet potatoes get crispy is to deep-fry them. But not anymore. Cut the sweet potatoes into thin match sticks or spiralize them into thin noodles. Cut them thin and, if you follow my other directions below, you will end up with crispy fries. Just make sure to watch at the halfway point so they don't burn. I like a little spicy topping, instead of overly sweet, so I created this syrup with heat to balance out the sweetness from the potato.

COOK TIME: 6 MINUTES ‖ SERVINGS: 2

2 large sweet potatoes

¼ cup (60 ml) maple syrup

1 tsp or more cayenne pepper

½ tsp cinnamon

1 tbsp (15 ml) extra-virgin olive oil (EVOO) to brush the basket and 1 tbsp (15 ml) more for the oil spritzer

Peel and wash the sweet potatoes. Make thin noodles using a spiralizer or cut them into thin matchsticks; thinner cuts will make them crispier. Soak the cut sweet potatoes in cold water for at least 30 minutes and change the water when it gets cloudy. Drain the sweet potatoes, pat them dry with a kitchen towel and spread them out on a cooling rack for about 10 minutes to dry them out even more.

Meanwhile, make the feisty drizzle by combining the maple syrup, cayenne and cinnamon in a small bowl and set aside.

Preheat air fryer to 360°F (182°C).

Brush the basket with EVOO. Fill the oil spritzer with EVOO and spray the sweet potatoes evenly and very lightly. Place the sweet potatoes in the basket and set the timer for 6 minutes. Shake or move the pieces around at 3 minutes. When the timer goes off, transfer them to a plate. Drizzle the potatoes with the maple sauce and serve immediately.

Note: If the sweet potatoes are thicker cuts than matchsticks, cook longer until done.

Yuca AU GRATIN

How many of you miss potato au gratin? (Raises hand.) I do. I miss the gooey and cheesy scalloped potatoes. But since we don't eat cheese, this recipe became one of our favorites. And yuca is perfect for those who don't eat white potatoes! Yuca has resistant starch and it's a great substitute for white potatoes. The Paleo "Cheese" Sauce (page 184) is easy to make ahead of time and you can assemble the rest of the dish for a quick side dish. If you have a mandoline, it would be very useful to cut the yuca into thin slices, unless of course, you have mad knife skills.

COOK TIME: 18 MINUTES || SERVINGS: 2

---

1 (12" [30-cm]-long) yuca

2 cups (475 ml) Paleo "Cheese" Sauce (page 184)

1 tbsp (15 ml) melted ghee, to coat the dish

1 tsp sea salt

1 tsp garlic powder

1 tsp chopped, fresh parsley, for garnish

Peel the waxy yuca root with a sharp knife. Using a mandoline with a flat blade, slice the yuca about ⅛ inch (3 mm) thick to get about 2 cups (360 g). Place all the slices in a large mixing bowl and soak them in cold water for an hour. Change the water as soon as it gets cloudy. You may need to change the water several times during the hour.

This is a good time to make the cheese sauce and then set it aside.

If using an ovenproof deep dish, grease the bottom and sides with ghee. If using a cast-iron skillet, greasing is not necessary. Drain the water and rinse the yuca slices to wash the starch off as much as possible. Line the bottom of the deep dish or skillet with one layer of yuca, then cheese, then yuca, and finish with the remaining cheese sauce on top. Sprinkle the top with the sea salt and garlic powder.

Preheat the air fryer to 360°F (180°C).

Cover the dish or skillet with foil, place it in the basket and set the timer for 10 minutes. When the timer goes off, remove the foil and cook for 8 more minutes. When the timer goes off, garnish with parsley and serve immediately.

Note: If you don't have a mandoline, you will need a very sharp knife to slice through this very hard root, which could be challenging. Just for this dish, you may want to buy a mandoline. It will be well worth the investment.

CAULI-Tots

I remember eating tater tots like they were going out of style when I was growing up. But now, as a mom, I read the label and was shocked at all the non-potato ingredients in the package! So, I wanted to re-create the recipe but added cauliflower with white potatoes to lessen the carbs. The air-fried version is just as crispy and quick to make. Your kids will never know these were made with cauliflower and potatoes without all the unnecessary chemicals!

COOK TIME: 8 MINUTES || SERVINGS: 2

¼ head cooked cauliflower (10 oz [285 g])

2 cups (13 oz [370 g]) cooked potatoes, cubed

2 tbsp (10 g) cassava flour (I like Otto's Cassava Flour)

¼ tsp garlic powder

¼ tsp onion powder

1 tsp parsley

¼ tsp sea salt

1 tsp ghee

2 tbsp (30 ml) extra-virgin olive oil (EVOO), for spritzing

Put all the ingredients in a food processor except for the EVOO and blend until chopped, but not pureed. You want some texture so it's okay if there are some pieces in the mixture. If you don't have a food processor, finely chop the cauliflower and cooked potatoes, add the rest of the ingredients except for the EVOO and mix well. Scoop about 2 tablespoons (20 g) of the mixture and shape them into a cylindrical, tater tot shape. Place them on a platter and cover. Refrigerate for 15 minutes.

Preheat the air fryer to 390°F (200°C).

Take out the cauli-tots, spritz with the EVOO, place them in the basket and set the timer for 8 minutes. At 4 minutes, move them around and cook until the timer goes off or until they are brown. Serve immediately with your favorite Paleo ketchup.

Vegetable TEMPURA

I will say this recipe was challenging to figure out for the air fryer, never mind trying to make them Paleo-friendly. But what's a good fried food cookbook without this quintessential Japanese tempura recipe, right? Well, you will be thrilled to know this is going to be a foolproof recipe. Just make sure to use potato flour and not potato starch. My kids devoured them, and I couldn't get them out of the air fryer fast enough! Try with various hearty root vegetables as well as cruciferous veggies like broccoli and cauliflower.

COOK TIME: 7 MINUTES || SERVINGS: 2

1 large egg

Unflavored seltzer or carbonated water

¼ cup (25 g) potato flour

1 zucchini

1 medium (4" [10-cm]-long) white Japanese yam or sweet potato

20 green beans

1 medium carrot

Extra-virgin olive oil (EVOO), for spraying

Ginger Dipping Sauce (page 188)

Beat the egg in a 2-cup (475-ml) measuring cup. Add the plain seltzer or carbonated water to the egg until you hit the 1-cup (240-ml) mark. Make sure the mark is for the liquid and NOT the foam on top. Slowly add the potato flour and mix well with a whisk. The consistency should be that of a thick custard. Add more seltzer water until the mixture reaches the 1½-cup (350-ml) mark. You may see little clumps, but that's okay. Pour the batter into a bowl and set aside.

Wash all the vegetables. Cut the zucchini in half widthwise. Then cut each piece in half, lengthwise. Cut each of those in half lengthwise again, and you should have a total of 8 pieces. Cut the carrots similarly, until you have similar-sized pieces, regardless of how many pieces you are left with. The important point is to have similarly sized vegetables, in general, so they cook evenly. Wash the Japanese yam well and, with the skin on, slice it into ¼-inch (6-mm)-thick slices.

Divide the vegetables into 4 batches. It's best to fry the same vegetables together since their thickness and density is the same. Coat them with the batter and shake off any excess. Place them on a plate and refrigerate for 10 minutes.

Preheat the air fryer to 360°F (180°C).

Spray the basket with oil to prevent the batter from sticking. Place the vegetables in the basket and spread them evenly. Set the timer for 7 minutes. If you want the outside to be crispy, spritz the vegetables with EVOO after 2 minutes. Serve immediately with the Ginger Dipping Sauce (page 188).

Tostones WITH MOJO DE AJO

Many Latin American dishes come with fried plantains and there's a good reason why. Deep-fried plantains make not only a delicious side dish, but also, they contain resistant starch, so they are healthier than other starchy fried sides. We'd eat them as snacks but deep-frying them always made me stay away from making them. But the air fryer made it easy for me to whip up a batch in a jiffy. Serve with a garlicky oil called *mojo de ajo* and they will quickly become one of your favorite ways to add more vegetables to your family's dinner table.

COOK TIME: 15 MINUTES || **SERVINGS: 2**

1 green plantain

¼ cup (60 ml) extra-virgin olive oil (EVOO), divided

2 cloves garlic

1 tsp finely chopped jalapeño pepper

1 tbsp (3 g) chopped fresh cilantro, plus more for garnish

1 tsp sea salt

½ lime, for garnish

With a sharp knife, cut both ends of the green plantain and score the skin lengthwise in two opposite sides. Peel the skin, and slice into ½-inch (13-mm)-thick disks. Put the disks in a medium-sized mixing bowl, drizzle 1 tablespoon (15 ml) of the EVOO and coat them well.

Preheat the air fryer to 390°F (200°C).

Place the plantains in the basket and set the timer for 5 minutes.

Meanwhile, to make the mojo de ajo, heat the rest of the EVOO in a small saucepan on medium heat. Add the garlic and cook until brown but not burnt. Add the jalapeño, cilantro and sea salt. When the cilantro wilts, turn the heat off and set aside.

Place a sheet of parchment paper on the cutting board. When the timer goes off, place the plantain disks on the parchment paper in a single layer. Cover them with a second sheet of parchment paper. With a meat tenderizer, flatten the disks. Place the flattened plantains back in the air fryer, set the timer for 10 minutes and continue to cook. When the timer goes off, place the plantains on a plate, drizzle with mojo de ajo liberally, squeeze lime juice and garnish with extra cilantro. If needed, sprinkle extra sea salt on top. Serve immediately.

Note: The greener the plantain, the more starchy and less sugary it will be, and it will hold up better in the air fryer. If it's starting to get yellow, it will cook very fast and may burn because it is more sugary. You can double the recipe very easily by making double the mojo de ajo and using two plantains.

Quick AND EASY FRIED PICKLES

The first time I saw this on a menu, I literally LOLed. I mean, seriously? But on a whim, I made this in the air fryer, and I was hooked. The hardest part was to make the darn crumbs stick to the slippery pickle chips, but when I succeeded, they were so good. Now I'm not laughing anymore. I'm too busy eating this quirky fried veggie. The moral of the story? Don't knock it until you try it at least once.

COOK TIME: 6 MINUTES || SERVINGS: 2

½ cup (50 g) cassava flour (I use Otto's Cassava Flour)

½ cup (30 g) Italian Breadcrumbs (page 187)

2 large eggs, beaten

2 cups (300 g) sliced dill pickles (1″ [2.5 cm] thick)

Extra-virgin olive oil (EVOO), for spritzing

Place the cassava flour and breadcrumbs on separate plates. Put the beaten eggs in a shallow bowl.

Coat the pickle slices with cassava flour, dip them in eggs and coat them with breadcrumbs. Make sure to coat all sides. Place them on a platter and when all the pickle slices are coated, cover the platter and refrigerate for at least 30 minutes. Take them out of the refrigerator and coat them with the breadcrumbs again, ensuring all the areas are completely covered. It's okay to wet them with some pickle juice or water so the breadcrumbs will adhere to the pickles.

Preheat the air fryer to 390°F (200°C).

Place the pickle slices in the basket and set the timer to 6 minutes. At 3 minutes, spritz the slices with EVOO, and check to make sure the pickle slices are being cooked evenly. When the timer goes off, take out the pickle slices and serve immediately with either Paleo ketchup or Horseradish Ranch Dipping Sauce (page 192).

Note: The trick to getting the flour and breadcrumbs to stick to the pickle slice is to keep the dry ingredients completely dry without clumps that may form from wet hands or tongs. So, do not use the same hand or tongs for the eggs and the flour.

Veggie CROQUETTE

Growing up, I remember biting into a hot croquette, crispy on the outside and soft on the inside, just out of the fryer. I liked the taste of the ingredients but didn't like the squishy oil texture. I reinvented the recipe for the air fryer and let me just say, I think this is much better than the deep-fried versions I tried in my childhood. If you haven't tried a croquette before, you'll be hooked.

COOK TIME: 10 MINUTES ‖ **MAKES: 6**

¼ head (140 g) steamed cauliflower

2 medium (14-oz [400-g]) cooked potatoes or sweet potatoes

¼ cup (50 g) finely diced carrots

¼ cup (50 g) finely diced zucchini with skin

1 tbsp (3 g) chopped fresh parsley

½ tsp sea salt

2 tbsp (10 g) tapioca flour

1 tsp garlic powder

3–5 tbsp (20–30 g) potato flour, as needed

½ cup (30 g) Italian Breadcrumbs (page 187), or more as needed

1 tbsp (15 ml) extra-virgin olive oil (EVOO), for spritzing

Place the cooked cauliflower in a food processor and pulse a few times until the florets become small, about the size of rice. Transfer them to a cheesecloth or a clean cotton kitchen towel and squeeze out the liquid as much as you can. Put them in a medium-sized mixing bowl. Put the cooked potatoes in the food processor and pulse a few times until smooth. Add them to the mixing bowl with the cauliflower. Add the rest of the ingredients except the breadcrumbs and EVOO. The mixture should be like a dry biscuit dough, so add the potato flour 1 tablespoon (6 g) at a time, accordingly. When the carrots and zucchini get cooked, they will create moisture, so you can make the dough a bit hard. Mix and shape them into oval-shaped balls and coat the outside with breadcrumbs. Place the balls on a plate and refrigerate for 10 minutes.

Preheat the air fryer to 360°F (180°C).

Take out the croquettes and spritz the outside with EVOO. Place them in the basket and set the timer for 10 minutes. At 5 minutes, move them around to ensure they cook evenly. When the timer goes off, serve immediately with either Donkatsu (page 63) or Paleo ketchup.

Buffalo CAULI-BITES

I went to college for two years in upstate New York where the locals ate Buffalo chicken wings by the barrel. I always wondered what happened to the rest of the chicken after serving all those wings. But I digress . . . These Buffalo Cauli-Bites are a take on the iconic food that made Buffalo, New York, so famous. The wings are usually deep-fried and then mixed in hot butter sauce, but this recipe calls for frying the cauliflower florets twice for better flavor. You can adjust the amount of hot sauce to your taste. And of course, you can use this recipe for chicken wings, too.

COOK TIME: 12 MINUTES || SERVINGS: 2

1 cauliflower

1 tbsp (15 ml) extra-virgin olive oil (EVOO)

2 tbsp (10 g) cassava flour (I use Otto's Cassava Flour), divided

4 tbsp (60 ml) melted ghee

3 tbsp (45 ml) Frank's Hot Sauce, plus more if desired

RANCH DRESSING

1 cup (235 ml) Homemade Mayo (page 180)

⅓ cup (75 ml) full-fat coconut milk yogurt

1 tsp garlic powder

1 tsp onion powder

½ tsp sea salt

1 tsp apple cider vinegar

1 tsp dried dill

Cut and discard the outer leaves and cut the cauliflower into florets. In a medium mixing bowl, mix the florets with EVOO and coat them with the cassava flour.

Preheat the air fryer to 360°F (180°C).

When the air fryer is ready, shake off any excess flour from the florets, place them in the basket, and set the timer for 6 minutes. Meanwhile, combine the excess flour, ghee and Frank's Hot Sauce in the same mixing bowl and set aside.

In a small bowl, make the ranch dressing by mixing all the ingredients, then refrigerate. When the timer goes off, transfer the florets to the mixing bowl and coat them well with sauce. Put the florets back in the basket and cook for 6 more minutes. Take them out when the timer goes off and add more Frank's Hot Sauce if needed. Serve immediately with the ranch dressing.

Saturday SAMOSAS

There is an Indian restaurant in my neighborhood, and every time I pass, the deep-fried samosas smell wafting through the neighborhood always makes me hungry. So of course, when I started to write this cookbook, I had to create this traditional Indian appetizer for the air fryer. The idea is to fill the dough with the traditional potato filling with delectable spices, but if you don't eat potatoes, you can use cauliflower mash and it'll work just as well.

COOK TIME: 15 MINUTES + 11 MINUTES STOVETOP COOKING || SERVINGS: 4

1 medium russet potato or sweet potato (about 9 oz [255 g]), quartered

2 tbsp (30 g) ghee

¼ cup (40 g) chopped onion

¼ cup (40 g) diced carrot

½ cup (75 g) broccoli floret ends or green peas

1 tsp curry powder

1 tsp garam masala

½ tsp turmeric

1 tsp grated fresh ginger

½ tsp sea salt

½ tsp black pepper

½ cup (20 g) chopped fresh cilantro, plus more for garnish

1 large egg white, beaten

1 tbsp (15 ml) extra-virgin olive oil (EVOO)

CRUST

½ cup (50 g) arrowroot flour

½ cup (50 g) extra fine blanched almond flour

¼ tsp salt

¼ tsp curry powder

1 large egg

Boil the potato for 8 minutes or until it is "just" done. In a medium mixing bowl, crumble the potato but do not mash. Set aside. Add the ghee to a frying pan and sauté the onion, carrot and the very ends of the broccoli florets for 3 minutes until soft. Add the crumbled potato and the spices and herbs. Mix everything, turn the heat off and set aside.

Set aside 2 sheets of parchment paper. To make the crust, combine the ingredients and divide into four balls. Place one ball in between the parchment paper and roll the dough out to a circle about ¼ inch (6 mm) thick. Fill the dough with the filling and shape it into a triangular-cone shape with one flat side. If there are any rips on the dough, smooth them out and close them. Repeat with the rest of the dough balls. Brush the outside of the samosas with the egg white wash and place them in the basket, brushed with EVOO.

Preheat the air fryer to 360°F (180°C).

Set the timer for 15 minutes. Check at 6 minutes to make sure they are baking evenly. Bake until the timer goes off. Garnish with cilantro and serve immediately.

Healthy ONION RINGS

I know you bought this book just for this recipe. I get it. And here it is. But I warn you, this is going to be addicting. I didn't think I'd love onion rings this much until I tried the air-fried version. The lightly breaded batter makes the savory and sweet flavor of the onion stand out so much more than the deep-fried method.

COOK TIME: 6 MINUTES || SERVINGS: 2

2 large onions, sliced in 1" (2.5-cm)-thick rings

½ cup (50 g) cassava flour (I use Otto's Cassava Flour)

2 large eggs, beaten

½ cup (30 g) Italian Breadcrumbs (page 187)

Extra-virgin olive oil (EVOO), for spritzing

Separate the sliced onion layers into single rings. Wash them, shake off excess water and set aside. This will help the cassava flour to stick to the rings. Place the flour and breadcrumbs on separate plates. Put the beaten eggs in a shallow bowl.

Coat the onion rings with cassava flour, dip them in the eggs and coat them with breadcrumbs. Make sure to coat the insides. Place them on a platter and when all the rings are coated, cover the platter and refrigerate for at least 30 minutes.

Preheat the air fryer to 390°F (200°C).

Scatter the onion rings in the basket, one over the other. Set the timer for 6 minutes. At 3 minutes, spritz the onion rings with EVOO, and make sure all the rings are being cooked evenly. When the timer goes off, remove the onion rings to a plate and serve immediately with Horseradish Ranch Dipping Sauce (page 192).

Note: The trick to getting the flour and breadcrumbs to stick to the onion rings is to keep the dry ingredients completely dry without clumps that may form from wet hands or tongs. So, do not use the same hand or tongs for the eggs and the flour.

 Fried AVOCADOS

Whoever thought of frying avocados was a genius. In fact, the harder and more unripe the avocado, the better. Make the Italian Breadcrumbs on page 187 and make this ASAP! Why wait in agony for them to ripen for other recipes when you can use them to make this now?

COOK TIME: 5 MINUTES || SERVINGS: 2

1 unripe avocado

½ cup (50 g) cassava flour (I use Otto's Cassava Flour)

½ cup (30 g) Italian Breadcrumbs (page 187)

1 large egg, beaten

1 tbsp (15 ml) extra-virgin olive oil (EVOO)

Cut the avocado in half, take out the pit and peel and cut each half twice, making a total of 8 pieces. Place the flour and breadcrumbs on separate plates. Put the beaten egg in a shallow bowl.

Coat the avocado pieces with cassava flour, dip them in egg and coat them with breadcrumbs. If the breadcrumbs don't stick well, dip the avocado pieces in the egg batter again and coat them again with breadcrumbs. Make sure to coat all sides. Place them on a platter and when all of them are coated, cover the platter and refrigerate for at least 30 minutes.

Preheat the air fryer to 390°F (200°C).

Place the avocado wedges in the basket and set the timer for 5 minutes. At 3 minutes, spritz the avocado pieces with EVOO, and check to make sure the avocado wedges are being cooked evenly. When the timer goes off, take out the avocado wedges and serve immediately with either Paleo ketchup or your favorite salsa sauce.

Note: The trick to getting the flour and breadcrumbs to stick to the avocado is to keep the dry ingredients completely dry without clumps that may form from wet hands or tongs. So, do not use the same hand or tongs for the eggs and the flour.

DECADENT FINALE

Life is short. Eat desserts first. Don't agree with me? Fine. But let me warn you: When you taste these desserts, you won't want to eat main dishes first ever again.

Pumpkin Coconut Crème Brûlée (page 150) will astound you because you made it in an air fryer. And roasting chestnuts in the air fryer alone is worth buying the machine, especially when you can make Roasted Chestnut Parfait (page 155) with them. See? There's a method to my madness. Glad you stayed with me. And since people always ask me how to eat persimmons, I thought it would be fun to make Persimmon Cobbler (page 152), especially since the season is only a couple of months in the fall. Who says a cobbler is only for peaches and apples? A cobbler is a decadent way to eat persimmons. While coconut macaroons are easy to make traditionally, popping them in the air fryer with this rich, maple-flavored recipe (page 144) is a quick way to make desserts everyone will love.

Chocolate-COVERED COCONUT MAPLE MACAROONS

If there is one Paleo dessert I could eat all day, it's coconut macaroons. And with my twist on this classic snack, quickly made in the air fryer, I am in trouble. It's a good thing coconut is good for you, ammaright? Indulge and make batches of this nourishing snack for everyone. Or just for you.

COOK TIME: 10 MINUTES + 2 MINUTES STOVETOP COOKING || MAKES 10–12 MACAROONS, DEPENDING ON THE SIZE

2 large egg whites

2 cups (150 g) coconut flakes or shredded coconut

¼ tsp sea salt

¼ cup (60 ml) maple syrup

2 tbsp (30 g) coconut oil, divided + 1 tbsp (15 ml) melted for the basket

1 tsp vanilla extract

CHOCOLATE DIP

6 tbsp (40 g) raw cocoa powder

¼ cup (60 ml) unrefined coconut oil

4 tbsp (60 ml) maple syrup

1 tsp vanilla extract

2–4 tbsp (30–60 ml) water

Beat the egg whites with a hand-held beater or a whisk until soft peaks form. Add the coconut flakes, sea salt, maple syrup, 1 tablespoon (15 ml) of coconut oil and vanilla. Fold the mixture into the egg whites until everything is mixed in. Refrigerate for 30 minutes.

Preheat the air fryer to 360°F (180°C).

Brush the basket with the remaining melted coconut oil. Spoon out a heaping tablespoon (10 g) of the mixture into your hand and roll it into a ball. Place it in the basket and repeat.

Set the timer for 10 minutes and cook until the timer ends or until they are brown. Cool them on a rack before serving.

Meanwhile, boil 2 to 3 cups (475 to 710 ml) of water in a saucepan. Line a baking sheet with parchment paper and set aside.

Place a glass mixing bowl large enough to sit on the saucepan without touching the water. Combine all the chocolate dip ingredients except the water in the glass bowl. Stir slowly for 2 minutes. Add the water to the glass bowl, 1 tablespoon (15 ml) at a time, until the chocolate dip becomes like a syrupy consistency. When the chocolate syrup is creamy and smooth, dip the macaroons in and then place them on the parchment paper–lined cookie sheet to cool. When all the macaroons are dipped in chocolate, refrigerate them for at least an hour, or until the chocolate is hardened.

Pumpkin RAISIN CUPCAKES

Pumpkin and raisins are a combination that doesn't need an introduction. They are quintessential fall ingredients for baked goods and together, these cupcakes will please children of all ages. And they are nourishing and naturally sweet! Make a few dozen for the lunch boxes. Of course, reserve a few for yourself, too.

COOK TIME: 10 MINUTES || SERVINGS: 12 SMALL OR 8 MEDIUM

PUMPKIN SPICE

3 tbsp (20 g) cinnamon

2 tsp (5 g) ground ginger

2 tsp (5 g) ground nutmeg

1½ tsp (4 g) ground allspice

1½ tsp (3 g) ground cloves

CUPCAKES

1 cup (235 ml) pumpkin puree

1 cup (95 g) cassava flour (I like Otto's Cassava Flour)

⅓ cup (80 g) ghee, softened at room temperature

2 tsp (5 g) pumpkin spice (see above)

½ tsp blackstrap molasses

1 tsp baking soda

1 tsp apple cider vinegar

1 tsp vanilla extract

½ cup (120 ml) maple syrup

½ cup (75 g) raisins

First, make your pumpkin spice. Then, combine all the ingredients for the cupcakes in a large mixing bowl and mix well.

Preheat the air fryer to 330°F (165°C).

Fill 12 silicone cupcake cups ¾ full and place 6 cups in the basket. Bake for 10 minutes, until they are brown or when the toothpick comes out clean when inserted in the middle. Repeat with the rest of the cups until all of them are done. You can either frost with your favorite frosting or eat them plain.

Note: Make the pumpkin spice and store in an airtight container for many of your fall baking needs.

Simple CHOCOLATE MUD CAKE

Don't let the list of ingredients scare you—this is actually a simple cake to make. The avocado chocolate frosting is so amazing no one will know this is a Paleo cake, even the non-Paleo cake snobs. A chocolate cake recipe can't get any simpler than this!

COOK TIME: 35 MINUTES || SERVINGS: 6

1 cup (100 g) cassava flour (I use Otto's Cassava Flour)

1 cup (110 g) unsweetened cocoa powder

¼ tsp baking soda

¼ tsp sea salt

¾ cup (175 ml) raw honey

½ cup (120 ml) avocado oil

1 tsp vanilla extract

¾ cup (175 ml) almond milk

¼ tsp apple cider vinegar

2 tbsp (10 g) collagen protein powder (not collagen peptides), or gelatin

3 tbsp (45 ml) hot water

1 tbsp (15 ml) ghee, softened

FROSTING

1 ripe avocado

½ cup (55 g) unsweetened cocoa powder

2 tbsp (30 ml) maple syrup

½ tsp vanilla extract

2 tbsp (30 ml) avocado oil

In a medium mixing bowl, combine the cassava flour, cocoa, baking soda and salt. In a large mixing bowl, mix the honey, avocado oil, vanilla extract, milk and apple cider vinegar. In a small bowl, combine the collagen powder and hot water and mix well. When the collagen powder is completely dissolved, add to the bowl containing the liquids and mix well. Slowly add the dry ingredients, in thirds, to the large bowl of liquids until all the dry ingredients are mixed well. The batter should be like thick mud, hence the title. Grease a round pan big enough to fit in your air fryer basket with ghee.

Preheat the air fryer to 360°F (180°C).

Pour the batter into the pan and cover with aluminum foil. Place the pan in the basket and bake for 25 minutes. Then uncover and bake for 10 more minutes, or until a toothpick comes out clean when inserted into the middle of the cake.

Meanwhile, make the frosting. Peel the avocado and cut it in half, take out the pit and add it to a food processor. Add the remaining ingredients and blend well until the consistency is a smooth texture. When the cake is done, place it on a cooling rack for about 15 minutes for it to be cool enough to decorate. When cooled, frost the cake and serve!

Note: This cake is not overly sweet, but if you'd like it to be sweeter, you can add ¼ cup (45 g) of coconut palm sugar to the dry mixture. Do not use more maple syrup or honey, or the liquid will make the cake too moist and it may fall apart.

Pumpkin COCONUT CRÈME BRÛLÉE

Who would think to make a pumpkin crème brûlée in the air fryer? You and I, of course. And with coconut cream, this classic decadent, but nourishing, dessert will make everyone think you slaved over the oven for hours. If you have a kitchen torch, caramelize the sugar on top to make it as dramatic as you can. Why not? You deserve the applause.

COOK TIME: 60 MINUTES || SERVINGS: 4

PUMPKIN SPICE

3 tbsp (20 g) cinnamon

2 tsp (5 g) ground ginger

2 tsp (5 g) ground nutmeg

1½ tsp (4 g) ground allspice

1½ tsp (3 g) ground cloves

CRÈME BRÛLÉE

2 cups (475 ml) full-fat coconut cream

½ cup (120 ml) pumpkin puree

1 whole vanilla bean, split lengthwise, or 1 tsp vanilla extract

1 tsp pumpkin spice (see above)

5 large egg yolks

½ cup (95 g) coconut sugar (fine or regular)

2 tbsp (25 g) coconut or turbinado sugar for torching, optional

Make the pumpkin spice by combining the ingredients.

In a saucepan, add the coconut cream, pumpkin puree and whole vanilla bean and bring to a simmer on low-medium heat while stirring gently until thoroughly mixed. Add the pumpkin spice and stir. Once it starts to steam, take out the vanilla bean and place it on a plate. Scrape off the beans from inside and add them to the pan. If you're using vanilla extract, add it at this time. Stir again until everything is mixed. Turn off the heat and let it cool for about 5 to 10 minutes.

Meanwhile, in a small bowl, whisk the egg yolks and sugar together. Once thoroughly mixed, slowly add about ¼ of the cream mixture to the yolk mixture while whisking. Next, pour the egg mixture into the rest of the cream mixture in the saucepan and mix it well.

Preheat the air fryer to 330°F (165°C). Crème brûlée needs to cook in a water bath and not in direct heat so find four bowls big enough fit your ramekins. Pour the crème brûlée mixture into each ramekin and cover them with aluminum foil. Carefully, put each ramekin in a bowl and fill the bowls with water just below the ramekin rims. When the air fryer reaches the desired temperature, carefully place the bowls with ramekins in the basket. You should be able to fit two bowls at a time. Set the timer and cook for 30 minutes. When the timer goes off, carefully remove the ramekins onto a rack to cool and remove the foil. Place the remaining two bowls in the basket and cook in the same fashion. When they are done, cool all the ramekins completely and refrigerate at least 4 hours or overnight.

You can serve them right out of the refrigerator, or you can sprinkle coconut or turbinado sugar on top and caramelize it with a kitchen torch.

Persimmon COBBLER

Okay, friends. Let me introduce you to this "exotic" seasonal fruit. I grew up eating this fruit but only recently have the local markets started to carry them. Maybe you saw them at your grocery store but didn't know how to eat them? I'll tell ya. You can wash them and eat them whole, or you can bake with them, like in this cobbler. After trying this cobbler, your family will want you to add this to your fall baked goods repertoire from now on.

COOK TIME: 15 MINUTES || SERVINGS: 2

FILLING

2 cups (300 g) peeled, sliced Fuyu persimmons

2 tbsp (20 g) raisins

1 tbsp (15 ml) raw honey

⅛ tsp cinnamon

⅛ tsp ground nutmeg

1 tsp ghee

¼ cup (60 ml) water

¼ tsp arrowroot flour

COBBLER TOPPING

½ tbsp (3 g) extra fine blanched almond flour

¼ cup (25 g) coconut flour

¼ tsp baking soda

½ tsp cinnamon

1 tbsp (15 ml) ghee, room temperature (soft but not liquid)

2 tsp (10 ml) raw honey, divided (I usually use 1 tsp of honey first and then measure out the remaining 1 tsp later)

½ tsp vanilla extract

Place the sliced persimmons in a small saucepan and add the raisins, honey, cinnamon, nutmeg and ghee. Simmer until the persimmons are limp but not too soft. Meanwhile, mix the water and arrowroot to make a slurry. Add the arrowroot mixture to the saucepan until the liquid is syrupy. Turn the heat off and let the mixture cool. Meanwhile, make the cobbler topping by mixing all the dry ingredients in a small mixing bowl. Add the ghee, 1 teaspoon of honey and vanilla. Using a silicone (or any flexible) spatula, mix the dry and wet ingredients until thoroughly moistened. Add the remaining honey to the mixture. Using the back of the spatula, press the ingredients and honey against the side of the bowl, forming a soft dough-like consistency. Set aside.

Preheat the air fryer to 360°F (180°C).

Transfer the persimmon mixture into two ramekins. Top each ramekin with the cobbler topping loosely, leaving some spaces for the mixture to bubble over as it cooks. If there are any loose granules of the mixture, press them into the persimmon mixture as you don't want dry ingredients to fly all over the place in the air fryer. Don't ask me how I know.

Place both ramekins in the air fryer, set the timer for 15 minutes and check around 8 minutes to make sure the top is not burning.

When the timer goes off, take out the ramekins and place them on a cooling rack for 15 minutes. You can put Paleo whipped cream or ice cream on top before serving. Personally, I like it "as is" because I think it's sweet enough.

Roasted CHESTNUT PARFAIT

This recipe came about after I discovered how easy and fast it is to roast chestnuts in the air fryer. Then, a light bulb went on in my head to make a chestnut cream. Then I wanted to bake with it. You see where I'm going with this?

COOK TIME: 20 MINUTES + 15 MINUTES STOVETOP COOKING || SERVINGS: 6

CHESTNUT CREAM

1 lb (450 g) chestnuts

1 cup (190 g) coconut sugar

3–4 cups (710–945 ml) water, divided

¼ cup (25 g) extra fine blanched almond flour

1 egg yolk

2 tbsp (30 ml) full-fat coconut milk

COCONUT CUPCAKES

¼ cup (25 g) coconut flour

⅛ tsp baking soda

3 large eggs

¼ cup (60 ml) coconut oil

2 tbsp (30 ml) raw honey

1 tsp vanilla extract

Wash the chestnuts in cold water a couple of times until the water is somewhat clear. Then, with a sharp paring knife, carefully slit each chestnut along the vertical line.

Preheat the air fryer to 360°F (180°C). Place all the chestnuts in the basket and set the timer for 10 minutes. All the shells should be opened. Take the chestnuts out to cool on a cooling rack. When cooled, peel the chestnuts and put them in a small saucepan. Add the coconut sugar and 2 to 3 cups (475 to 710 ml) of water to immerse all the chestnuts. Turn the heat to medium, bring to a boil and then simmer on low heat for 15 minutes or until chestnuts are tender. Remove the pan from the heat and let cool for 10 minutes. Take a few chestnuts out and chop them into small pieces for the topping. In a food processor, add the remaining chestnuts and about 1 cup (235 ml) of the water. Process for about 3 to 4 minutes until a thick cream forms. If it's too thick, add more water. Add the rest of the ingredients and process until all the ingredients are well incorporated. Chill the cream in the refrigerator for at least 30 minutes.

To make the cupcakes, sift the coconut flour and baking soda together in a large mixing bowl. Add the eggs, coconut oil, honey and vanilla and mix well. Pour the batter into 6 silicone cupcake cups.

Preheat the air fryer to 360°F (180°C). Place the cupcake cups in the basket, set the timer to 10 minutes and cook until the timer goes off. When the cupcakes are done, take them out to a cooling rack to cool.

Slice the cupcakes into 1-inch (2.5-cm)-thick slices. Take out the chestnut cream and assemble the parfait. First, spoon the chestnut cream in the bottom of a parfait glass, add a cupcake slice and then scoop some more chestnut cream. Continue until the parfait glass is filled. Top with the chopped chestnut pieces before serving.

BARE NECESSITIES

In order to make many of the recipes in this cookbook, you'll need to make some of the basic recipes in this section first, hence the title. For example, you should make the Baked Potatoes (page 158) for the Stuffed Chipotle Potato Skins (page 72); Eggs Three Ways (page 167) for Kimchi Deviled Eggs (page 19) and Stuffed Chipotle Potato Skins (page 72); Roasted Garlic (page 171) for Filet Mignon with Herbs and Roasted Garlic (page 52) and Roasted Garlic Aioli for Chicken Tenders with Roasted Garlic Aioli (page 84). Make the Paleo Biscuits (page 164) for the breadcrumbs in many breaded recipes. Tortillas or Tostadas (page 176) will be needed for Huevos Rancheros (page 22) and Fish Tostadas (page 103). But you don't have to use them just for this cookbook. They are perfectly fine as sides for your own recipes, too.

Baked POTATOES

How long do you bake potatoes in the oven? 40 minutes? 60 minutes? Well, if you have an air fryer, it'll be done in half the time or less. And when you can make Stuffed Chipotle Potato Skins (page 72), you'll want to bake a few in advance. Poke a few holes with a fork, and no need to wrap them in aluminum foil either!

COOK TIME: 15–32 MINUTES || SERVINGS: 1

1 potato

1 tbsp (15 ml) extra-virgin olive oil (EVOO) for coating the potato skin

1 tsp sea salt

1 tsp fresh chopped parsley or sprouts, for garnish

Wash the potatoes well. Using a fork, poke the potatoes all around. Coat the potato skin with EVOO. It has a low smoking point and the highest temperature an air fryer goes up to is 390°F (200°C), so it's safe to use. Coating the potato skin lightly with EVOO will make the potato skin crispy. Sprinkle with sea salt and garnish with parsley or sprouts before serving.

COOKING TIMES FOR DIFFERENT SIZED POTATOES:

Small—5–7 oz (140–200 g), cook for 15 minutes
Medium—7–9 oz (200–255 g), cook for 22 minutes
Large—9–11 oz (255–310 g), cook for 32 minutes

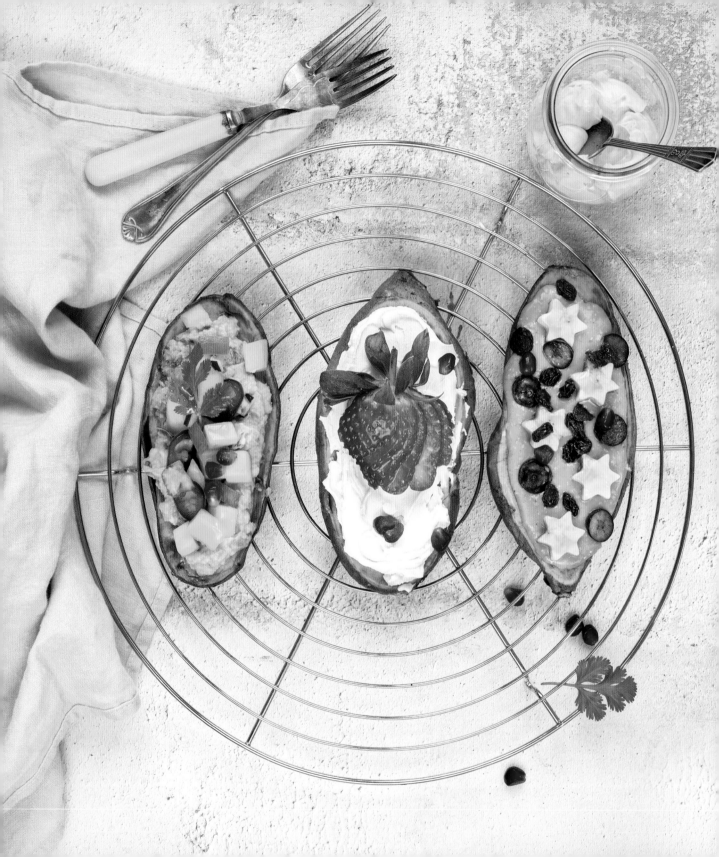

SWEET POTATO *Toast*

Since wheat bread toast is off the menu, sweet potato slices have replaced the wheat toast in my house. Making these in the air fryer is easier than using the toaster, too.

COOK TIME: 10 MINUTES || 2–3 SLICES OF TOAST PER MEDIUM SWEET POTATO

1 sweet potato

1 tbsp (15 ml) melted ghee or avocado oil

Wash the sweet potato and pat the skin dry with a paper towel or kitchen towel. Set aside to dry a bit more. Slice it lengthwise, about ¼- to ½-inch (6- to 13-mm) thick. Brush both sides with fat—ghee or avocado oil.

Preheat the air fryer to 360°F (180°C). Place the sweet potato slices in the basket in a single layer. Set the timer for 10 minutes. You don't want them to turn to mush; they should be just firm enough but cooked. You can smear them with more ghee, dip them in maple syrup, drizzle them with honey or add protein toppings.

Cashew BUTTER SWEET POTATO TOAST

I used to have peanut butter and banana sandwiches as a kid when there was nothing to eat in the house after school. I thought I'd re-create a similar snack with a healthier twist. I substituted peanuts with homemade cashew butter and added raisins. This may become your child's favorite after-school snack!

COOK TIME: 10 MINUTES || MAKES: 3 SLICES OF TOAST

1 cup (150 g) raw cashews, soaked

3 tbsp (45 ml) water

Pinch of salt

3 slices of toast from a medium sweet potato (recipe above)

1 cup (150 g) banana slices

½ cup (75 g) raisins

Put the soaked raw cashews in a high-power blender. Blend until the cashew butter is thick in consistency, while adding the water 1 tablespoon (15 ml) at a time. Depending on how thick you want the consistency to be, you may need to adjust the amount of water. Add a pinch of salt to taste. Smear the cashew butter on the sweet potato toast, add the banana slices and top with raisins.

Guacamole WITH MANGO SALSA TOAST

Guacamole and mango salsa could make my stomach do the tango. I love having them together in salads or on sweet potato slices. And they make great toppings on caramelized toast. You'll be addicted. I guarantee it.

COOK TIME: 10 MINUTES || MAKES: 2–3 SLICES OF TOAST

GUACAMOLE

1 ripe avocado

¼ cup (50 g) diced purple onion

1 tbsp (15 ml) lime juice

¼ cup (10 g) chopped fresh cilantro

2 tsp (6 g) minced garlic

1 tsp sea salt

½ tsp black pepper

MANGO SALSA

1 cup (150 g) diced mango

½ cup (80 g) diced tomato

¼ cup (50 g) chopped purple onion

½ of a jalapeño pepper, chopped, or 1 tablespoon (10 g) diced jalapeño pepper

¼ cup (10 g) chopped fresh cilantro (reserve 1 tsp for garnish)

2–3 slices of toast from a medium sweet potato (page 161)

To make the guacamole, cut the avocado in half, take out the pit and save it. Scoop out the avocado into a small bowl and add the onion, lime juice, cilantro, garlic, sea salt and black pepper and mix well. Place the avocado pit back in the guacamole, cover and refrigerate while you make the mango salsa.

Combine all the ingredients for the mango salsa in a small bowl. Take the guacamole out of the refrigerator, spread it on the sweet potato toast, top with the mango salsa and garnish with cilantro before serving.

Strawberries AND CREAM
TOAST

I don't know anyone who doesn't like strawberries and cream. You don't know either, right? Then try this toast. You're going to wonder why you didn't think of making this before. Promise. This toast is like dessert rather than a morning toast.

COOK TIME: 10 MINUTES ‖ MAKES: 2–3 SLICES OF TOAST

1 (13.5-oz [383-g]) can full-fat coconut milk

½ tsp vanilla extract

Sweetener of your choice, e.g. maple syrup, coconut palm sugar or honey

2–3 slices of toast from medium sweet potato (page 161)

2 cups (300 g) sliced strawberries

Refrigerate the can of coconut milk for 24 hours. You can also use coconut cream, which is thicker and has more cream than liquid. At least 24 hours after it's been chilled—without shaking—open the can and scoop out the thick cream at the top of the can into a medium bowl. Leave the milk behind for other cooking uses like in soups and sauces. You should have enough to make 1 cup (235 ml) of whipped cream. If you are using coconut cream, you should definitely have enough.

Using a handheld beater, whip up the mixture until soft peaks form. Add the vanilla and sweetener of your choice and beat until incorporated. Spread the whipped cream on the sweet potato toast and top them with sliced strawberries before serving.

Paleo BISCUITS

This was one of the earliest recipes I tried in the air fryer. I must have gone through at least 10 pounds (4.5 kg) of different types of flours before coming up with this perfect combination. These biscuits are amazing with warm ghee and jelly or drizzled with honey.

COOK TIME: 12 MINUTES || MAKES: 6 BISCUITS

½ cup (50 g) coconut flour

1 cup (95 g) extra fine blanched almond flour

¼ cup (25 g) tapioca flour

½ tsp baking soda

¼ tsp sea salt

¾ cup (175 ml) full-fat coconut milk yogurt

2 tbsp (30 g) ghee, room temperature

1 tbsp (15 ml) raw honey

2 tsp (10 ml) vanilla extract

½ tsp apple cider vinegar

Combine the dry ingredients in a medium-sized mixing bowl and sift. In a small mixing bowl, combine the yogurt, ghee, honey, vanilla and apple cider vinegar and mix well. Add the wet ingredients to the dry ingredients and mix until a dough forms. Do not knead too much; otherwise, the biscuits will be hard. Divide the dough into 6 small balls and shape them into 1-inch (2.5-cm)-thick round biscuits.

Preheat the air fryer to 360°F (180°C).

When the desired temperature is reached, place the 6 dough balls in the basket. Set the timer for 12 minutes. Check at 10 minutes to make sure they are browned but not burnt. Store in an airtight container.

 THREE WAYS

Cooking eggs in the air fryer sound as crazy as flying elephants. Okay, that might be a far-fetched analogy, but I thought it was that crazy until I tried it. And oh boy, air fryers can cook anything! Use the cooking time as a guide—you'll have to try a few eggs to get the hang of it since every egg is different in size, even if the carton says large or extra-large. The point is, you can cook eggs without turning on the stove top for a pot of water!

COOK TIME: 5–11 MINUTES

Large pastured eggs that are more than a week old

Place the eggs right in the basket in a single layer. Cook according to the timetable below for the different variety of eggs. For all the eggs, make sure the shells are not broken and are intact before cooking. Otherwise, the egg shells may crack while cooking in the air fryer and you will not be a happy camper. Also, you may want to turn the eggs upside down halfway through to avoid one side from turning brown. Once the timer goes off, immediately plunge the eggs into an ice water bath for about 5 minutes for easier peeling.

COOKING TIMES FOR DIFFERENT TYPES OF EGGS

Hard-boiled—11 minutes
Soft-boiled—8 minutes
Poached—Grease ramekins and preheat them to 300°F (150°C). Gently crack the eggs in the ramekins and cook for 5 minutes. I poach eggs in ramekins to place on top of food because it is easier to slide the eggs onto food than trying to crack the shells of delicate egg whites and raw egg yolks cooked directly in the air fryer basket.

BACONOMICS

Do you bake bacon in the oven? Me too. I will never go back to frying bacon on the stove top, to getting grease splattered all over the place. It turns out baking it in the oven gives me the same result; grease all over the oven for me to clean. Not very helpful. Enter the air fryer. I was amazed how easy it is to cook bacon in it and the cleanup is easy! I'm all for easier cleanup in the kitchen, aren't you?

COOK TIME: 14 MINUTES

12 strips uncured bacon without sulfites that are similar in thickness

You may need to try this a few times before you get the hang of making bacon in the air fryer. The cooking time may vary depending on the thickness of the bacon. It also depends on how many bacon strips you are making at once. While you don't have to lay them down in a single layer, it is important that you don't crowd the basket too much either. As the bacon starts to cook and get smaller, they will take up less space, but it's important not to crowd the basket. Usually, in the oven you can set the temperature at 200°F (95°C) and cook for 14 minutes for crispy bacon, but it may take a couple of minutes longer in your air fryer.

Also, they may not look "crispy" when they are done, but when you leave them out on a plate lined with paper towels, they will get crispy. Drain the bacon grease pooled in the bottom of the basket and reserve it for cooking! This is my favorite way to cook bacon now. No mess!

Roasted GARLIC

Truth be told, roasted garlic is like candy. So, when I found out it's quicker to roast it in the air fryer, I roasted as many bulbs as I could fit in the basket and used them up almost right away. Roasted garlic is not only great on pasta but also smeared on steaks, like in Filet Mignon with Herbs and Roasted Garlic (page 52), so roast as many as you can fit in your air fryer. You'll be glad you have a few on reserve in a pinch to use for recipes.

COOK TIME: 30–40 MINUTES

Whole garlic bulbs, as many as you need to roast or can fit in the basket

1 tbsp (15 ml) extra-virgin olive oil (EVOO) *per* garlic bulb

Wash the whole garlic bulb without peeling. Discard any loose skin but keep most of the outer layers of the skin intact. Using a sharp knife, cut the top of the bulb, exposing the cloves on top. Put it in a small bowl then drizzle the EVOO all over the exposed cloves, making sure to get the oil in between the cloves. Repeat for all the bulbs.

Preheat the air fryer to 360°F (180°C).

Cover the garlic bulbs loosely with aluminum foil. Place the bulbs in the basket and set the timer to 30 minutes. When the timer goes off, uncover the foil and check for doneness. If you can squeeze the cloves right out of the skin, then they are done. If not, put them back in the basket, uncovered, and cook for 10 more minutes or until they are soft.

Cauli COUSCOUS

You can make cauli couscous basically any way you want. You can steam it or bake it in the oven but honestly, steaming it creates more moisture that you'd have to squeeze out if you're making cauli mash, and it may be too soft for a couscous. Baking it in the oven is okay but why waste all that energy for one head of cauliflower? So, the air fryer is a perfect appliance to make cauli couscous! Cut them up into florets first so they will be cooked evenly and season according to your need, like Chicken Tandoori with Lime and Cilantro Cauli Couscous (page 80), right before serving. But however you serve it, don't call it "cauli rice" because it really isn't "rice." That's not nice.

COOK TIME: 17 MINUTES ‖ **MAKES: ABOUT 2 CUPS (460 G)**

1 head cauliflower

2 tbsp (30 ml) avocado oil or ghee

1 tsp sea salt

Cut the cauliflower into florets. Place them in a bowl and mix with the oil and sea salt.

Preheat the air fryer to 330°F (165°C).

Transfer the cauli florets to the basket and spread them out as much as you can. Set the timer for 17 minutes. Shake the basket or move the florets around halfway through. When the timer goes off, place the florets in a food processor and pulse a few times until all the florets are broken up to the size of couscous. Set aside to use them with recipes in this book or beyond.

Ground BREAKFAST SAUSAGE

Breakfast sausages are cheap if you want the chemical-laden commercial variety from stores. But this is honestly one of the easiest breakfast proteins to make at home. And when you have a fast cooking appliance like the air fryer, there is no reason why you should ever buy them. You can either make the loose sausage for recipes like Healthy Biscuits and Gravy (page 33) or make this mixture into patties and fry them in the air fryer. Either way, you'll never buy another commercial sausage again. You like them a little sweet? Add some maple syrup. There's no magic here.

COOK TIME: 10 MINUTES || MAKES: 2 CUPS (450 G)

---

1 lb (450 g) ground pork

2 tsp (5 g) garlic powder

1 tsp fennel seeds

1 tsp dried rubbed sage, or rub whole sage leaves in between your fingers

½ tsp dried thyme

1 tsp dried parsley

1 tsp sea salt

Mix all the ingredients in a large mixing bowl. Heat a frying pan over medium heat. Cook the sausage mixture, stirring constantly, for about 10 minutes, or until the pork is opaque. Set aside to be used in recipes.

Or make sausage patties and cook them in the air fryer at 360°F (180°C) for 10 minutes, or until brown.

Tortillas OR TOSTADAS

Grain-free tortillas are not only easy to make but they are easy to make into tostadas in the air fryer. If you have a tortilla press, you might think you are better equipped than I, but I beg to compare your tortillas to mine from the air fryer. Tostadas are great for Huevos Rancheros (page 22) and Fish Tostadas (page 103) since they are light and crispy. You can even cook this recipe a little longer and they'll become like chips! I love multi-purpose recipes, don't you?

COOK TIME: 3–5 MINUTES ‖ SERVINGS: 4

½ cup + 1 tbsp (55 g) cassava flour (Otto's Cassava Flour is what I use), divided

½ cup (50 g) extra fine blanched almond flour

¼ cup (60 ml) warm water

½ tsp sea salt

Sift ½ cup (50 g) of the cassava flour and the almond flour together in a medium-sized mixing bowl. Add the warm water and salt. Mix well and form a dough with your hands. Divide into 4 pieces and place the dough in between two floured parchment papers. Flatten them out with a rolling pin until you achieve the thickness you like.

Preheat the air fryer to 360°F (180°C). Place one tortilla in the basket, place a small rack over the tortilla and bake for 3 minutes. If you need tostadas for Fish Tostadas (page 103) and Huevos Rancheros (page 22), then cook them for 5 minutes until they are crispy. Cook the rest of the tortillas until all of them are baked.

BASIC STAPLES

This section is for sauces and dips that are needed as a marinade, like Teriyaki Sauce (page 183) for the Korean Beef Jerky (page 113) or Paleo "Cheese" Sauce (page 184) for Lobster Mac and Cheese (page 99). There are dipping sauces (pages 188–192) and essential Breadcrumbs (page 187) you can use for recipes in this cookbook and beyond.

Homemade MAYO

I never liked any food that required mayonnaise, until I made my own homemade mayo. After realizing how easy it is to make mayo, I've enjoyed all kinds of dips and salads that require mayo. And who would have known mayo is healthy! Make this in advance for various dips and sauces you'll need in this cookbook.

MAKES: 1½ CUPS (355 ML)

1 large egg

1 large egg yolk

2 tbsp (30 ml) lemon juice

1 tsp Dijon mustard

½ tsp sea salt

1 cup (235 ml) avocado oil

Combine all the ingredients in a wide-mouth mason jar or 2-cup (475-ml) measuring cup. Or you can use a tall container that will hold the ingredients and not splatter when blending with an immersion blender. If you don't have an immersion blender, why not? You need to buy one. Just kidding. You can always exercise your arm muscles and whisk briskly to emulsify the oil to a thick mayo.

When using the immersion blender, bring the blender wand up and down to incorporate all the ingredients and emulsify the oil. Slowly, the mayo will become thick and you'll have to move the wand a little slower. When the avocado oil is emulsified, and all the ingredients are combined, store the mayo in an airtight mason jar and refrigerate. Use within 2 weeks.

Teriyaki SAUCE

Teriyaki is a versatile sauce for making many Asian recipes. This sauce is without soy or gluten so it's safe to use in many recipes that require teriyaki sauce. This is the sauce used for Korean Beef Jerky (page 113) and Beef Negimaki (page 71) in this book. Make jars of it and use it in your family's favorite Asian recipes, too.

COOK TIME: 5 MINUTES ǁ MAKES: 1½ CUPS (355 ML)

½ cup (120 ml) water

1 tbsp (5 g) arrowroot flour

¾ cup (175 ml) coconut aminos

¼ cup (60 ml) raw honey

2 tbsp (30 ml) blackstrap molasses

½ tsp ground ginger

½ tsp garlic powder

¼ tsp black pepper

Add all the ingredients to a small saucepan and without turning on the stove, mix well with a whisk. When the arrowroot completely dissolves, turn on the heat to medium, and bring to a boil while stirring. When the sauce bubbles, lower the heat and simmer for 5 minutes while stirring. The consistency should be like a BBQ sauce. Turn off the heat and set aside to cool. When cooled, transfer to an airtight glass jar and refrigerate for up to 2 weeks.

Paleo "CHEESE" SAUCE

Since we don't eat dairy anymore, I created this cheese-like sauce using non-dairy ingredients and nutritional yeast for recipes that require gooey cheesy sauces. And I was introduced to nutritional yeast in the process. But I have to admit, working with nutritional yeast was a bit challenging since I didn't know what to expect. But for making a cheese sauce, it turned out to be the hero ingredient. Make this cheese sauce for the Lobster Mac and Cheese (page 99) and Yuca au Gratin (page 122). You will never look back to those cheese-y years. Sorry. Couldn't resist.

COOK TIME: 5 MINUTES ‖ **MAKES: 2½–3 CUPS (591–710 ML)**

---

2 cups (300 g) cooked cauliflower, about ½ head of cauliflower

½ cup (120 ml) full-fat coconut cream

1 tbsp + 1 tsp (10 g) nutritional yeast

½ tsp dry mustard powder

½ tsp dried tarragon

3 tsp (15 ml) ghee, softened at room temperature

2 tbsp + 1 tsp (14 g) arrowroot flour

¼ cup (60 ml) chicken stock

1 tsp black pepper

½ tsp sea salt

¼ tsp turmeric for color, optional

In a food processor, combine all the ingredients and blend until smooth. Transfer the mixture to a small saucepan and cook it over medium heat for 3 minutes until it bubbles. Reduce the heat and simmer for 2 minutes while stirring and scraping the bottom of the pan constantly, so the bottom of the pan does not burn. Adjust the amount of arrowroot and chicken stock for the "right" consistency as the sauce thickens. When it reaches the consistency of melted cheese, turn the heat off and cover until needed. If you are not going to use it right away, store it in an airtight glass container and refrigerate. Reheat on low heat before using.

BREADCRUMBS

This is more like a method than a recipe. First, you'll need to make biscuits and you can either make plain breadcrumbs or Italian-style breadcrumbs for more flavorful dishes. Either way, aren't you glad you can have breadcrumbs again?

COOK TIME: 12 MINUTES ‖ MAKES: 2 CUPS (120 G) OF BREADCRUMBS, OR 6 BISCUITS

1 cup (120 g) coconut flour

1 cup (120 g) extra fine blanched almond flour

¼ cup (30 g) tapioca flour

½ tsp baking soda

⅛ tsp sea salt

¾ cup (175 ml) full-fat coconut milk yogurt

2 tbsp (30 g) ghee, soften at room temperature

1 tbsp (15 ml) raw honey

2 tsp (10 ml) vanilla extract

½ tsp apple cider vinegar

Combine the dry ingredients in a medium-sized mixing bowl and sift. In a small mixing bowl, combine the yogurt, ghee, honey, vanilla and apple cider vinegar and mix well.

Preheat the air fryer to 360°F (180°C).

Add the wet ingredients to the dry ingredients and mix until a dough forms. Do not knead too much. Otherwise, the biscuits will be hard. Divide the dough into 6 small balls. Form into the shape of a biscuit 1 inch (2.5 cm) in thickness. When the air fryer is ready, place the 6 dough balls in the basket. Set the timer for 12 minutes. Check at 10 minutes to make sure they are browned but not burnt.

Place the biscuits on a cooling rack and loosely cover with parchment paper overnight. Put 2 to 3 biscuits in a food processor and pulse a few times until they become crumbs. Store in an airtight glass container until needed.

FOR ITALIAN BREADCRUMBS, combine 1 cup (60 g) of Breadcrumbs, 1 tablespoon (5 g) of Italian seasoning (equal ratio of dried oregano, thyme, basil, rosemary and marjoram) and 1 tablespoon (5 g) of garlic powder. Mix well and store in an airtight jar for up to 3 weeks at room temperature and up to 2 months in the refrigerator.

Ginger DIPPING SAUCE

I use this dipping sauce for everything. Okay, except for maybe chicken tenders or French fries. Or wait, maybe I should try it! Why not? Ginger is so good for you and dipping anything you can in this sauce is fine by me! But the sauce is especially good for Wonton Bites (page 16) or Vegetable Tempura (page 127). But seriously, try it with Fancy Pants French Fries (page 118). I dare you.

MAKES: ¼ CUP (175 ML)

1 tbsp (15 g) grated fresh ginger

½ cup (120 ml) coconut aminos

1 tbsp (15 ml) mirin or sake, optional

1 tbsp (15 ml) cold water if not using mirin or sake

Combine all the ingredients and store in an airtight container in the refrigerator for up to 2 weeks.

Spicy KOREAN DIPPING SAUCE

Korean food always requires something spicy and this dipping sauce will knock your socks off. Make it as spicy as you'd like and it'll just enhance the food you're dipping even more, like the Korean Dumpling Bowls (page 64). Try this sauce with other foods, too. Your taste buds will never want bland food again.

MAKES: 1 CUP (235 ML)

½ cup (120 ml) coconut aminos (tamari is okay if you tolerate it)

¼ cup (60 ml) cold water

1 tsp gochugaru

1 tsp toasted sesame seeds

1 tbsp (5 g) finely chopped scallions

1 tbsp (15 ml) rice vinegar, or apple cider vinegar if you are avoiding rice

Combine all the ingredients and store in an airtight container in the refrigerator for up to 2 weeks. Make the sauce in advance, so all the flavors are infused when using.

The dipping sauce can be easily doubled. Gochugaru can be found in any Asian or Korean grocery store, or on Amazon. But in a pinch, you can use red chili pepper or cayenne pepper.

Horseradish RANCH DIPPING SAUCE

The horseradish and mayo combination just screams fancy dip for fried foods to me. So naturally, this sauce can be served with any food in this book. But it's especially delicious with Quick and Easy Fried Pickles (page 131) and Healthy Onions Rings (page 139). It's also perfect with Crab Cakes (page 95) and Fish Tostadas (page 103). If you don't have pineapple juice to make the tropical dipping sauce, you can use this for Coconut Shrimp (page 107), too.

MAKES: ¼ CUP (60 ML)

1½ tbsp (20 ml) Homemade Mayo (page 180)

2 tbsp (30 ml) full-fat coconut milk yogurt

2 tsp (10 ml) apple cider vinegar

1 tsp onion powder

2 tsp (1.5 g) finely chopped fresh parsley

1 tsp finely chopped fresh chives

½ tsp sea salt

½ tsp black pepper

1 tsp grated fresh horseradish

Combine all the ingredients—adding the horseradish last—in a small bowl. Then, store in an airtight jar and refrigerate until needed or for up to one week.

TIPS FOR USING AN AIR FRYER

The air fryer is one of the most popular kitchen appliances. This small countertop kitchen gadget works by circulating hot air around the food at a high speed, frying, baking and roasting the food. It especially attracts those who don't want to deep-fry foods but still want food with a crispy outer layer. But because the air fryer uses less energy than a convection oven and less oil than a deep fryer, it is equally popular to anyone who wants to cook fast and serve healthy home-cooked meals. Food is cooked in a cooking basket that sits in a drip basket to collect any oil that is produced from the food. While using less oil may be desirable for some people, not all oil is bad if you know which oil to use. In fact, avocado oil and coconut oil are healthy for you, so use them liberally.

There are many models of air fryers on the market and most of them work similarly. I have a Philips Avance XL but these tips will be helpful regardless of which model you might have.

1. Place the air fryer in a well-ventilated area with no other flammable items nearby. Use a dedicated AC plug in the wall and do not use an extension cord. Do not plug in other heat-producing appliances in AC plugs in the same circuit. You will trip the circuit breaker.

2. Marinate meats. Because the food gets cooked rather quickly, they will need time for the flavor to be infused. When you are ready to cook, coat it with oil for a crispy finish.

3. It's best to use a meat thermometer to check for doneness.

4. Do not use aerosol cooking spray cans. Besides the fact that they are not healthy for you, they contain chemicals that will cause some air fryers' coating to peel and chip. Invest in an oil spritzer instead. You can find it at local kitchenware stores or on Amazon. The spritzer will evenly coat the food with the oil of your choice for a crispier finish without harmful chemicals for you or the air fryer. Fill it with either extra-virgin olive oil or avocado oil.

5. Spray the entire food evenly. Don't just spray the top or one side. If the food is fatty, like chicken with skin on, you don't need to spray all over. The skin will produce its natural oil to fry. Steaks or lamb chops are the same. Their natural oil will suffice so you don't need to spray them. But vegetables should be sprayed if you want a crispy finish, so spray evenly all over.

6. If you are using a flour-based breading, shake off the excess so the food is not left with dried flour after it's cooked.

7. Use parchment paper with holes (available at local Asian markets or Amazon) to line the basket for wet, battered food.

8. If the air fryer starts to smoke, it usually comes from the burning oil in the drip pan; so if you're cooking extra fatty meats, empty the drip basket intermittently. Use the air fryer near a vent or use it outside, like on your patio or in the garage, where smoke will not set off the smoke alarm. Don't use water to control smoking issues as some online tips may suggest. You'll end up steaming the food instead of frying.

9. Do not fill the basket up to the max line as the basket indicates. Keep the food more than 2 inches (5 cm) below the top of the basket. Otherwise, the food will burn since the heat source is on top.

10. Shake or flip the food to keep it from sticking to the basket, if needed. The Philips model has a stainless steel wire basket so there's enough air flow and it does not need to be shaken or flipped. But other models without a wire basket may require moving the food around for even cooking and to prevent it from sticking. Check the food halfway through the cooking time.

11. Keep your eye on the timing for cooking any food. Some things take less or more time than you think. Again, use the meat thermometer for meats to make sure they are cooked thoroughly.

12. To clean the baskets, leave the cooking basket inside the drip basket and fill them with hot, soapy water for a couple of hours or overnight. The grease and food particles will come right off. Do not use abrasive sponges. Use only non-abrasive soft sponges. Otherwise, you will scratch the surfaces and the finish will peel, chip or rust. It doesn't matter how often you cook oily food; always clean after using the air fryer. Otherwise, the machine will end up with baked-on grease, which will be harder to clean.

Note: I have the Philips Avance XL, which has a stainless steel wire basket. There are other models with a Teflon-coated basket with holes, which may chip and peel over time. I find stainless steel to be a better option than Teflon, which is coated with perfluorooctanoic acid (PFOA), a carcinogenic chemical. The walls and the drip basket for the Philips XL are coated with Teflon but the food does not touch them, and the maximum temperature goes up to 390°F (200°C), which is a safer temperature for PFOA to off-gas. There are bigger models that have removable trays, like a toaster oven, and if you have the counter space, that might work better for you. But know that the clean up will be a hassle, like an oven. Whatever model you purchase, do the research and buy the unit that fits your needs and can fit in your kitchen. Happy air frying!

ACKNOWLEDGMENTS

As a wife, mom and doctor, there is nothing more rewarding than cooking nourishing food from scratch that my family enjoys. But I made sure my children learned the power of food for health and where their food came from by visiting local farms and farmers' markets, and they even helped me grow food in our backyard. I am confident that this knowledge will enhance their health.

Blogging to keep recipes for my children to refer to has been a privilege. But writing a cookbook has been my goal to help more people heal with food. And it didn't happen without the help of so many people who were there for me.

My husband: I can't thank you enough for being so supportive. Your willingness to try new recipes with unfamiliar ingredients and new kitchen gadgets, like the air fryer, made this journey that much more fun. Thank you for washing endless mixing bowls and measuring cups, lugging groceries and paying for items that sometimes ended up in the garbage. Without you believing in my work, this book wouldn't even have started. I love you for that. Oh, and wipe the chicharrones crumbs off the side of your mouth.

My children: I know how much you suffered from allergies and eczema. And oh, how I wish I could be the one suffering instead of you and how I wish there were some magical foods I could cook to make your pain go away. Despite how some of my foods tasted, you were like the trusting, little, hungry birdies that just blindly open their beaks at the sight of their mom, regardless of what she brought in her mouth. Thanks for being my birdies and trying everything I made for you. And I appreciate how you thank me at every meal. You humble me and make everything I do worthwhile.

My mom and dad: Thank you for listening and asking if I need help. I hope I am half the parent that you are. I hope writing this cookbook made you proud of me. I love you both more than I can express in words, so I'll continue to cook all the holiday meals.

My in-laws: Thank you for having a son who is willing to try any food at least once. His gastronomic curiosity made this book possible, and I owe it to you for raising him with home-cooked meals from scratch. I hope I can perfect your drunken chicken soup soon.

Brad, Vince and Wendy: I know you had doubts, but I know deep down, you believed in me and rallied, "You've got this!" Thank you for trusting me and seeing me reach this goal. Love you!

Page Street Publishing: Thank you for having faith and throwing the ball at me. I hope it was worth the gamble. And thank you for answering my umpteenth questions without hitting delete, delete, delete and rolling your eyes. Lastly, thank you for supporting "The Trustees," a local land conservation and history preservation organization. This reason alone makes me proud to be part of the Page Street Publishing family. Our children, our future, thank you.

My blogging friends: Blogging can be lonely when you don't share an office with colleagues. But I have amazing online friends who support each other's work. Kelly Bejelly for accepting me as a member of the Primal & Paleo Group, Emily Sunwell-Vidaurri for always being my cheerleader and Amanda Torres for giving me tips on how the publishing process works. And those who encouraged me endlessly, you guys rock!

Jennifer Robins: Thank you so much for introducing me to Page Street Publishing. Without you putting your neck out for me, this book would have never taken off the ground. You're my "shero!"

My former partner in crime and BFF, Anna Hackman, for having so much more confidence in me than I! Without your constant support, as any Jewish mother would, I don't know if I could have kept pushing myself to become an author. Love you, sistah!

My friends from all walks of life who continuously encourage me, give me high fives and promise to buy my books. You are my biggest groupies! Thank you, and I love you!

Donna Crous, my new friend, confidant and photographer, who might have been separated from me at birth and placed on different continents: when I asked a Paleo community about a challenging recipe, you went out of your way to not only make it, but also to photograph it so artistically. You are a wickedly talented recipe developer and photographer. You don't know how deeply your generosity touched me. No wonder they voted you as the U.K. Paleo Blogger of the Year! I am so honored you accepted my request to photograph my book. As they say, we feast with our eyes first, so thank you, from the bottom of my heart, for helping my readers taste this book through your lens!

Last but not least, thank you to my loyal readers and followers. Without your reading and engaging on my blog and social media, the possibility of writing a cookbook would have never entered my mind. How wildly you reacted to my eCookbooks and emailed me about recipes led me to write this cookbook. Your thirst for nourishing food and passion for how to keep your family naturally healthy keep me researching and investigating continuously. Let's keep learning so we can be the pillars of our future generations' health. Thank you so much for your love and support for my work!

ABOUT THE AUTHOR

Dr. Karen Lee is an accomplished holistic practitioner, Doctor of Chiropractic and Acupuncture and Oriental Medicine Fellow. Dr. Karen treated patients with various ailments with standard chiropractic care, acupuncture, nutrition therapy and mind-body medicine before she retired.

Dr. Karen started writing about holistic health and real food recipes on drkarenslee.com after helping her children with numerous food allergies and sensitivities. She believes that many illnesses can be prevented or reversed with real food, proper nutrition, supplements and stress management. She also believes many of the health struggles can be managed effectively by adopting a whole food, real ingredient eating habit as a lifestyle and not as a mere temporary "diet." Dr. Karen shares allergy-friendly, ketogenic and Asian Paleo recipes that have helped many people across the world on her website drkarenslee.com. You can find her as @drkarenslee on social media.

INDEX